THE TRUTH THAT TEARS US
APART;
THE LIES THAT KEEP US
TOGETHER

THE TRUTH THAT TEARS US APART; THE LIES THAT KEEP US TOGETHER

A RELATIONSHIP BOOK

KENNETH KENNYTALK DEMOSS

iUniverse, Inc.
Bloomington

The Truth That Tears Us Apart; the Lies that Keep Us Together
A Relationship Book

iUniverse books may be ordered through booksellers or by contacting:

iUniverse
1663 Liberty Drive
Bloomington, IN 47403
www.iuniverse.com
1-800-Authors (1-800-288-4677)

ISBN: 978-1-4759-5312-1 (sc)
ISBN: 978-1-4759-5313-8 (ebk)

Library of Congress Control Number: 2012918310

Printed in the United States of America

iUniverse rev. date: 10/27/2012

CONTENTS

INTRODUCTION

This is book is dedicated to all the mistakes I have made in my life as it pertains to dealing with the opposite sex. These mistakes help me understand where I have been and help me appreciate the lessons I have learned. They are a major part of who I am and they also help me share this gift that was given to me.

To the ladies that didn't give me the time of day or realized that I was not the one for them and left me alone. You helped me understand that I could not tell every chick the exact same thing trying to gain sex. They also help me understand that I needed to take care of my business and not focus on trying to have sex with every chick that I met. It made me focus on my craft, my talent and all the people I could serve with it.

To the players and pimps that I have watched, that I have listened to and learned from when I was a young child trying to find his way through sex, love, and heartbreak. You helped me realize my ability to attract ladies which helped me to gain the experience after dealing with women from all walks of life.

To The father figures in my life that was there for me with insight on dating and dealing with girls throughout my time in school and most of my adulthood. They gave me the courage to talk to females, taught me how to talk to them, and taught me not to be afraid to losing them.

To The rap artist that I listened to growing up that did make attempts to shed light on not being a sucker for females and helping us recognized when they only had gold digging tendencies. They pointed out the silly things that guys were doing in the name of getting a girl to have sex with them or to simply be their girlfriend.

They all helped shape who I am today, Kenneth Kennytalk DeMoss.

Hello Fellow Readers: Lend me your ears, eyes, mind, and hearts, along a journey through my thoughts, my point of view, my take on situations, as well as my side of the story that has not been told before. This is a chance to hear a different angle on many of the familiar situations that you may have never heard before. It is for entertainment purposes only, however through being entertained you can be educated.

The truth that tears us apart is that which we hear and see daily yet choose not to acknowledge out of fear of losing someone you care about. Fear of how that special someone would react to us pointing it out, or fear of falling into the category of a failed relationship that people on the outside may criticize you for. Fear that the info we hear from other failed relationships are true about our own. The key word you heard in this paragraph is fear. It causes us to react blindly to things we know and see. Which brings us to the lies that keep us together, the very opposite of what we see. We choose to believe and see things a certain way to keep a comfortable lifestyle, a happy home, a successful relationship, or the envy of all relationships. We all want to be seen as being on the right track, making the smartest decision and a step ahead of others in life. So we hear and see the truth, ignore it and change it to a lie just as long as it keeps us together.

I am not a licensed physician, I don't have a degree in psychology, but I do have a story. This story, when people hear it gives me the ability to speak on situation about the heart because unlike many, I have had experience with an amazing amount of women in my life. The difference is that

I have paid attention and learned something from each of them. I'm not going to go deep into my story because at this time it is not about me. It's about you and the confusion that is experienced on the dating scene, in relationships and in marriages that ends in heart break, divorce and even worse. Many will try and get you to focus on the messenger instead of the message to distract you. Please, don't be distracted from what is finally here to remove a veil from your eyes in an entertaining manner and help you get your spirit and emotions under your control.

I wanted to reach out to the world and give it a treasure that will transcend this generation and be around for our grand kids. I don't want them falling for the same things we fell for; I don't want them going through what we went through due to lack of knowledge, wisdom and understanding. There are many things that I could focus on in my life but I wanted to do something for the people. Relationships are the most common thing in life, we all would like to have but obtaining it in the manner we would like, can become a confusing rat race that many feel they can't win. The dating shows, the fairytale weddings, the slow songs about happiness and unhappiness, the merry go round of love. Before we could begin to win, we first need to focus on the small components of relationships, dating and courtship as it was called back in the day. We have to take it back to elementary school, and back to the neighborhoods we grew up. The TV shows that influenced us and last but not least, the emotions themselves.

I know there are several books that have been written by several relationship experts, and I feel they deserve the chance to write their books and be exalted to the level of their accomplishments; however, that's not why I am writing this book. I am writing it because I feel I was chosen to step out on faith and make this happen. I feel like I tried to ignore it for a long time but situations in my life did not allow me to run any longer. Like the young troubled kid in the projects that did everything under the sun in sin, yet still found his way to the pulpit to become a preacher. I know my credentials bring questions but like it states in the scriptures, God will bring someone from the level of everyone to get a job done. The meek will dumbfound the wise is what it says.

I come from amongst you from a perspective that all will be able to relate. I will share with you some truths that we choose to ignore at times for the reason of helping you figure out the game of cat and mouse.

This book was written for 3 major reasons in my life that I will share with you. The first reason is a beloved brother, Alvin Holmes. We use to talk about relationships that we were involved in at the time, sharing insight to help each other. These talks turned in to us venting to each other, as well as sharing information that shined a light on our situations. One day I was giving him some insight on a situation and the information I provided really hit home with him and he revealed an idea to me he wanted to work on. He advised me how interesting my take on relationship situations were, and said we should team up and write a book. This will be a cool way to share our thoughts with the world. I thought this was cool, and I was really interested. But at this point in my life, I was not interested enough to start it the project with him as of yet. He did tell me that he did start taking notes on the book and he wanted to share some with me, but I couldn't find the time in my busy life to start. A few years passed, and unfortunately, so did my brother suddenly. He passed way the young age of 41 and this left me heartbroken; however, it also struck a fire under me to start and complete this project. I was always a writer so this transition was fairly easy. Due to his untimely demise, I felt compelled to complete this in his honor, dedicating it to the memoir of a good dude.

Number two is the feedback I have always gotten about my perspective on issues, and subject matter. When I think back about the people I have met, and the impact I had on them, based on mere conversation, I realized that this could be a universal way to express myself unlike anyone else on the planet. There are people from my past that I would speak to in the present, who remind me of things that I said, how it impacted them, and how it was such truth to it. I felt that the "jewels" that I possess must be shared because not sharing them would not help the world. I realize that I want to use this to entertain, but like comedians, their experiences, word choice, and insight gives us a humorous way to look at everyday life situations. It also provided ways to view and handle them.

This book is the perfect platform for me to express myself, because unlike other ways I used to express myself such as music, that I love as well, these projects could be overseen by me and only me without any outside influences. This brings me into reason number 3, which is just, my passion to express myself. I have recorded music over half of my life trying to get into the music industry. I realize that due to my situations that I involved myself in, I never had complete control. So my ideas get morphed and shaped into something else by the time it's recorded due to producer, A&R or CEO involvement. This is the best way to express myself in which I vowed not to involve any one. So ladies and gentleman, these are my thoughts, my perspective from my lifelong experiences with relationships with the opposite sex. These are my lesson learned with knowing people who have gone through situation I have helped them with or I have learned from the mistakes they have made. Not only speaking about relationships of the opposite sex but also of the same sex, due to me having people I have met from the gay and lesbian communities. This is about relationships in general because we are all human and even if we don't agree, we must acknowledge that we struggle with the same situations and behaviors when it comes to the disease called "Love" closely and always confused with "Lust". Walk with me on this journey, and prepare to laugh, learn, debate, disagree, as well as relate, agree, and pick up insight. Prepare to be entertained, from a young kid coming into his own to an adult, handling adult issue in relationships.

WHAT IS THE #RELATIONSHIPTRUTH?

I realized at this point, with all of the insight I had, all of the lesson I had learned and the honesty I was inspired to uphold, I had come up with a way of thinking. This way of thinking lead to me speaking and providing insight in a manner that I had never heard anyone before. It's reminiscent of a relationship consultant or expert but not exactly. A relationship expert or counselor provides advice based on the information they gain while probing and listening to you. What I realized that I was blessed with was not that, but it was the ability to see truth in relationships. A relationship is two people going through a series of situations and circumstances and what makes the relationship last is how they communicate or deal with these situation and circumstances. So what I was doing was providing people about the truth about their situation or circumstance and allowing them to make the decision on the action to take. The best way to ensure people make the best decision, they have to have the truth about the situation. Truth is going to outlast any illusion, or misrepresentation that lives in a relationship. I feel that I had to bring this truth in relationships to more than the people that I came across in my personal life, but to the world. I felt compelled to do this through a vehicle that I had never attempted before, in the form of a book. At that very moment, my philosophy called #RelationshipTRuth was born.

When you can recognize the #RelationshipTRuth, it helps you understand which advise to take from a relationship counselor or expert. It helps you make decisions clearly and optimistically. It's also an unbiased look from all angels which leads to an unbiased decision made, void of emotion. The lack of emotion ensures its honesty and consideration for all party involved. This is the #RelationshipTruth.

THE TRUTH THAT TEARS US APART, THE LIES THAT KEEP US TOGETHER

By Kenneth KennyTalk DeMoss

What you are about to read is going to change your world. It's very simple, first you read the book and it may take you to a place you are familiar, giving you a different way to look at that situation. This unique way of looking at a familiar situation will spark a level of growth in you helping you handle these situations more effectively. Or you will read this book and it will take you to a place you are not familiar, and in short, it will do the exact same thing, when you get to the situations described. Furthermore, with your world, his world and her world changing, there's only a matter of time that this book changes the whole world! So, I recommend you fasten your seat belts and keep your arms inside of the ride.

I say this because in the day and time we are living, it is time for things to be said that many have feared over the years. It is time to talk about situations in relationships between us as humans that many feel are taboo, or just plain mean, due to the way it may impact someone's feelings. The reason that we cannot move forward in our knowledge of relationships as well as us moving towards true happiness in relationships is that we are so focused on our emotions and our selfish approach to relationships.

I felt that this book would be the ideal way to express myself, because with my dealings in and around the music business, there is little creative control without a proven record as well as money. When I expressed myself, the ideas would be morphed and shaped into another person's vision by the time it's recorded. When you hear it, it is not what I, the writer envisioned. With writing, I can say what I feel without having anyone's input on what they feel I should talk about.

These are my thoughts and perspective from a long life of relationships, and experiences with love and infatuations. Lessons learned from people I have helped along the way or from the mistakes I made on the road to becoming a man without a solid male figure in the house. It goes even deeper, to focus on the human side of relationships so that the gay and lesbian community will be able to relate. We must understand that we are all people and we go through the exact same things. We must all admit that we struggle with this disease we call "love", closely and almost always confused with lustful attraction.

Walk with me on this journey and prepare to laugh, learn; debate; disagree, as well as relate; agree and pick up insight. For the moment I have your attention, remove all blindfolds and listen closely. Think about what I am saying and remove emotion. When emotions are added, they prevent you from seeing what is right in front of you. They hinder you from becoming a more aware version of yourself, which is what is needed for you to make the transition to whatever you strive to be in this world. Intimate relationships are the back bone of our existence, and are vital to everything we do in this world. For example, many of us don't function well when our "love life" is not going so well. Even when we experience success in our professional life, and we don't have anyone to share it with or there are problems in the relationship at home, there is still no happiness. I will touch on this more throughout the time we spend together and I hope that when you are done, you sell it or give it to someone else so that it reaches everyone.

I need everyone to understand that this book is not for a particular gender but for the good of both. Through my perspective and views, I will expose men and women to the truths about each other they see but choose to ignore. Exposing what we don't see that hinders us from growing together or being happy apart. I will help women to understand what level we are on at the time we meet and in our lives so they understand clearly how to deal with us. I will help men see the level that women are on and how to deal with them which is strangely not so different from us. I'm going to start by speaking of the main two schools that we go through as men and women so that we understand the basics and this will help us live together in harmony. This book is the cure for painful break ups and divorces. It's the cure for domestic violence, infidelity as well as the expectations we set on each other that we often times don't live up to. I will tell you story of the Hunter and the Fisherman and how we all go through these schools at different parts of our lives. The key is to be able to identify this and handle accordingly.

I will tell you the story of the Hunter and the Fisherman, from my perspective to give you vivid picture of how you can compare it to situations in your life. I will tell you the thought pattern as well as the actions and reactions of people going through these schools. It may offend some, it may help others, but the goal is to entertain you with insight and create dialogue around things we shy away from discussing.

I have never understood why we become so consumed or involved with a person. Well, I understand the initial reason we hook up or gravitate towards with each other. The feeling that you get when you see that special someone who is attractive, who gives you that look of interest, and nature takes its course. However, after the first few encounters of sensual seduction, heated touching and soft wet kisses, the thrill starts to leave the building. When this happens, the two individuals have become used to having each other around and an unspoken relationships takes place. We are now "seeing each other" as we call it. This is the point where exclusivity is assumed and we just seem to fall in a girlfriend and boyfriend situation. Now when this happens, we find ourselves keeping other at bay while he or she is around. We keep the phone on silent or don't answer calls out of respect, which gives them feeling that you want this relationship with them. We start having to answer to them as to where we going, who we are going with and how long will we be there.

At this point, we find ourselves in situation where we think we want to be, until we go hang out with the girls or the guys again. The same circumstances you met your new significant other under, you find yourself in again. This is where things get weird, because you glance around the bar or the club while sipping on your drink and you see another pretty or handsome face, looking back at you. This face gives you a similar feeling your significant other gave you when you met before the feeling started to fade.

The dedicated person you are trying to be, steps in and you walk away out of respect for your new situation. This happens the next few times that you are out on the town, however the more you are out, the slower your walk away out of respect becomes. You find yourself holding casual conversations, to dancing, and grabbing a bite to eat afterwards. All these are completely innocent, so you tell yourself. The more you stick with your significant other the more you want to hang out and continue your innocent activity. This activity starts to become more comfortable to you, to the point where what happens during these innocent activities are never discussed with your new companion. The reason why is because "it's no big deal" and there is "no need to discuss thing that just may make the other person jealous." The behaviors that we implement while out with our friends become looser, flirtier, more private, and kept away from our new partners.

As time pass with our new relationship, our significant others start to want more time with you and it starts to cut into the time you spend out on the town. We go along with it for a while only to start lying to get away and hang out. This continues to happen until, yes, you guessed it, you get caught and have to answer for lying and for being where you didn't advised them you would be. Frustrations start to set in because after a while, we start to resent the situation due to it restricting us from what we really want to do. Arguments start until you realize that this was a big mistake.

We should have ended this situation sooner. We knew earlier that the thrill started to leave but we said nothing. We continue to see this person because we felt obligated to each other due to the things that were done sexually. The things that were told to each other during our connection and the way we made each other feel. This clouds our thinking, leading us into a situation we really don't want to be in. Situations like this normally bring children in the world, engagements to be married as well as bitter break ups and divorces. It all starts from that first look, that connection that is made between two people. This connection should have started and ended on a great note, and not be allowed to form into what it is simply not. It should not be forced in a direction that it shouldn't go in. A one night encounter should be just that because we have a certain respect for the person afterward. Contrary to what we believe, when you see a person that you have had a one night encounter with, you appreciate them for not complicating your life. There are some who wish that it could have been more who may feel different, and some who wish it hadn't happened because the sex was not fulfilling, but overall there is a respect.

This is what is needed in the relationships between adults, and the only way to achieve is by being honest with our feelings. This is a difficult thing to do, because of the concern that we have for each other's feelings. We are so concern about each other's short term feeling that we forget and think nothing of the long term feelings. Like lying to someone or going alone silently watching a relationship happen that you do not want to be in.

This is the origin of many relationships. Though there are many that start off with one night stands or with us getting emotionally carried away, many last long periods of time and that is the beauty in all of this. We can never tell the outcome but we hold on during the journey hoping it turns out for the better of us both. It is not easy to be together so being together does turn into a fight for what you have. I think these fights are necessary due to one of us loving the other more, or so they feel; or one of us allowing this strong emotional state we are in to cause them to make changes the other one does not want. These are changes that one of us may not be ready to make so quickly, due to feeling comfortable the way things are. There is always someone in the relationship that has the direction all figured out, and takes the lead to ensure that the relationship is exactly what they feel it should be. These are the people, men or women, that find themselves trying to convince the significant other that what they feel and the vision they have will be best for the union. I think we have all been that person before and I have two words for that person in the relationship. "Shut up." You must shut up and do more listening to what your significant other thinks, and if they don't mention any thoughts, ask them for their thoughts before you suggest anything. This is where we have to recognize when selfishness starts to set in our thoughts and we drive towards what is most pleasing to us instead of our partners.

These are points that will be touched on in the following sections so read with an open mind, and with the intent to be entertained. Listen to the message, the point of view and the insight, leaving all emotions out of it. Emotions are the reason we make decisions we know we should not make. We hope things don't turn out the way we know they are going to turn out before making decisions due to our judgment being clouded by emotions. Kennytalk is here to give all that I have learned to all those who are willing to read and accept. This is only to create dialogue around what we need to be talking about as adult that are involved everyday with situations of the heart. Follow me on this journey and let's change the world together, one world at a time, starting with your world.

THE HUNTER

Wherever you are, I will find you. If you fit the description, If you are the flavor that I savor, If I sense you are near, with my keen sense of smell, hearing or given in sight, I will attack sounds a lot like a stalker, huh? But no, I'm am not a stalker, killer, Rapist, or Pervert. I am a growing male with a strong sometimes-uncontrollable attraction for the opposite sex.

At the sight of a pretty face, enticing physique, legs, cleavage, shoulder, stomach, collarbone, lips, beautiful hair, revealing attire, smooth skin, eyes, and last but not least a nice ass, I'm lock in. I'm loaded and ready to shoot. Sex is truly a weapon that I will use within a blink of an eye. If you are in my range, you will be shot. At the grocery store shopping, you will be shot; at the library studying, you will be shot; out taking a stroll, you will be shot; working hard on your job you will be shot; when you walk out of the comfort of your home, you will be shot.

This shooting behavior manifest in several ways which could range from taking a double look at a female or starring, unwanted physical contact such as grabbing your arm to get your attention or worst. This may make many women/ladies feel uncomfortable, sad, or frustrated. The very thought of not being able to go about your life without constantly being preyed upon, sounds freighting. However, this may sound intriguing to some women. The thought of your vanity being glorified, not only when you look in the mirror, but where ever you go, dispute what you are doing or what you're wearing is heaven on earth. This, along with the thirst to hunt, motivates my behavior.

The feeling can start from anywhere in my body, but always ends with the penis. This point in my life, I wanted to express my emotions with my penis. Women sometimes confused this period of my life as being immature and labeled me as a dog. All men don't go through this promiscuous period, but the ones that do, it can be a great school to go through. There are Pros & cons.

GRADUATING CLASS

This period can be known as the period in which I learned every aspect of women. I have the benefits of dealing with women of all walks of life, which helped me over stand exactly what women want. This also helps me become a better provider of what women want, as well how to recognize when to provide it. Women are a beautiful species that have many of the same wants and needs, but have several different ways they want or need it to be given to them. This school helps me over stand way to deliver.

The school of the hunter helps me do what many believe prevents men from commitment or a monogamous relationship. It allows you to "Sew my royal oats", or getting promiscuous intentions out of my system. Therefore have a desire to settle or slow down. The cons consist of maximum exposure of different women sexually increase the chance of diseases. There are many of my peers that enroll in the school of the hunger, but flunk out or drop out with diseases that affect them the rest of their lives. These chances can be minimize with uncompromised use of protection and contraceptives. This leads directly into the chance of possibly fathering children early in life. With going through the school happen mainly at a young age, this leads to underage father who are not aware of what it takes to raise a man, due to us not being men as of yet.

There is also the possibility that you do not graduate from this school. Some of us remain in this state due to the addiction to the pleasures and freedom the school provides. There are responsibilities that come with being in the school, but not the responsibility of answering to anyone. I can see who I want when I want, with no strings attached.

The key to graduating this school is to over stand that there is an important rule that you have to follow, that is openly communicating with your partners. This prevents misunderstandings as well as feelings being hurt with unspoken or false expectations. This is the perfect time to be honest and open with your partner due to us not having a reason to lie. However, there are reasons that we still take the dishonest or unspoken road in this school.

The first reason is that this attraction, as I explained earlier can be uncontrollable. With uncontrollable feelings come uncontrollable behaviors and actions. Some of are so addicted and focused on the sexual thirst for our partner, we say and agree too many things we truly don't mean. The female species are emotional individuals with clear ideas of what they want their encounters and relationships to look like. They set indirect or soft expectations that turn out to weight more than we can lift. Guys can relate that the beauty of a woman can distract you from seeing these signs and clues they try to get across to us. We tell them what they want to hear, allow them to think whatever they want, to get what we want. This leads to expectations not being met; promises not kept and hurt feelings.

The next reason stems from the fact that it's in our nature to take care of you and protect you. It's in our nature to console, and cherishes the woman. These truths about us do not manifest in the way that proves this to the ladies. The way we express this care is not in the most obvious way. These feelings are also expressed at different times and at different level we are on while playing the dating game. A guy will not be honest in a relationship due to his fear of knowing how the truth will affect his partner. It has been said many times by women, "be man enough tell us the truth" however we all know what happens when we are totally honest. Total honesty hurts feeling, so we do our best to avoid hurting the girls' feelings.

In the school of the hunter it is totally about the male or female sewing their wild oats as they call it.

It's an aggressive stage of dating where the individuals on this level are consumed by a sexual drive.

"When I was a player, I walk, talked, and thought as a player; when I became a man, I saw that I was more than a player"

Wherever my friends and I went, they knew I would leave with a phone number. I had a classy, professional, and smooth way of approaching young ladies. It wasn't obnoxious, or aggressive, and it was successful 85% of the time. Armed with confidence, and the ability to respond, I was totally focused on being the valedictorian of the school. There were several one-night stands, and hundreds of sexual encounters from hundreds of women. I was a true player playing the game.

Let me tell you a short story of a hunter that was similar to me. We can call him young fella, and I would like to allow you a peak in on the lifestyle he lived. It was about staying fly, talking fly, and conquering as much pussy that he could. Sisters, mothers, daughters, have all had the common denominator, him between their legs. He was a handsome brother, short and charismatic, blessed with gift of gab. He used it to add as many ladies as he could to the infamous list. This guy could have sex with a fine lady, wash up, go to the club and try to meet another girl to spend the night with. A young man that was addicted to the orgasm, as well as giving orgasm, was right at home in this school.

Young fellow was blessed in this spectacular way, however was not blessed when it came to the financial level he was raised. Born in the ghetto he naturally attracted young ladies, from all financial levels. He enjoyed pleasing each girl that he came in contact with sexually. Young fellow's behavior was observed by an old—timer that was concerned and wanted to give him some game. He reminded young fellow about current situations, and how his behavior did nothing to improve it. The old-timer point out the level of girls he involved himself with, and who was truly benefiting from their encounters. Young fellow gave them good dick, made them feel very special and spent countless amounts of, what the old timer called precious pimping time on them. He motivated them to be better at what they did or what they wanted to do. And they gave him nut. The old timer said that young fellow could "beat his dick" or masturbate and get the same feeling. This young fellow also had a very special lady that he truly had feelings for, but was too selfish to tell her of the life he truly led. From this young lady perspective, she was frustrated with dealing with a guy who showed her he cared, but hid an important aspect of his life from her. She had no idea of the school he was in, but knew she did not completely have him to herself.

This lack of communication, and honesty through time created bitterness in this young lady. The phone numbers that she found, the information she received from friends that reported what they saw young fellow doing or heard he was with. The countless arguments follow by passionate nights of makeup sex.

The encouraging talks and the lonely nights; the quality time he spent with her and his constant running the streets, the promises of growing old together and the countless girls that she had to deal with "claiming" to have slept with her man. These behaviors pushed her away and pulled her closer at the same time. Inconsistency leads to confusion, confusion leads to frustration and frustration leads to bitterness. Bitterness is a cancer that can spread to anyone near you or who listens to you. Young fellow could have avoided taking this young lady through this by just having honest communication. If she had been educated on the school of the hunter she would have understood what he was going through and been able to make a clear decision if she wanted to stay around. After countless bitter conversations with her friends, whom are now bitter, she gave young fellow an ultimatum. She wanted him to settle down at his 25 years of age, stay out of the streets and night clubs. She wanted his commitment that the girls and the rumors of girls stop or he would lose her forever. He was not ready at this time and was not actually listening to the old timers' observations of him. He also knew that he cared for this young lady deeply, and he felt that he may never meet another one that made him feel the way she did. So he did give in and agreed to marry her to show his commitment to her and his fear of losing her. He made her the happiest women in the city.

Now, we all know that happiness is a state of mind, not a place or an accomplishment so the marriage did not last long. He had not yet finished the school of the hunter and was eventually up to his old ways. He was addicted to pleasing the girls and woke up one morning to find he was in a marriage, only to please this one young lady. She now realized that young fellow may have been the person for her but this was definitely not the time. This brought her to the conclusion of staying with him and accepting him as he is at this time or divorce. Children were involved so this complicated the situation even more. All because of the lack of honest communication and the lack of understanding of the school of the hunter, the impact on couples and families can be major. The moral to the story is with a more in depth understanding of this school; we can fix an emotional, social, and mental problem that comes from relationships that have gone wrong. The understanding of the school of the hunter can eliminate so many issues in society.

THE FISHERMAN

I heard a man say, when asked about the type of women that he like, he stated, "I like women who like me". This wise man was a father figure to me, Carl Ivy who at the time he advised me of this. I really did not grasp what he was saying but hindsight is clear as water, and I gained a clear understanding of this at an early age. This mindset or way of thinking is described as being a "fisherman". It separates you from so many guys in the game that is on the prowl for the opposite sex. The hunter is a very large school that many of us don't ever really graduate from. They possess the perception that we as men must, and have and always will be the aggressors. Women have been programmed and raised to be prepared for these encounters, as a mother gazelle prepares her baby gazelle for the lions and tigers. This is what makes the fisherman so unique and intriguing to the female. The behavior men display gives us a desperate persona, but being a fisherman aligns you with the woman, because this is exactly how many women think. They are strategic, when choosing from the many options that come their way, and with 90% of men being the aggressor; they have plenty to choose from.

The hunter has to set traps, wait patiently for his prey to come. When the prey comes, they make their strike. If they don't bull's eye, which men as the aggressor do 80% of the time, the chase is on. The prey is running, ducking, jumping and dodging to get away from you. If the prey is caught in the game we play, the prey calls the shots. We become so fascinated with the beauty of our prey that we jump through hoops to become whoever they want us to be, or who they are comfortable with.

This is done to get them to like, want, or deal with us. We are happy anyway we can get it. This puts the prey in control throughout the encounter, which allows total control even over thoughts, and behaviors while in the presence of the prey. Situation like this gave birth to females Mack's, who understand how to play the game of pussy" keep away" long enough, or strategic enough to squeeze out an abundance of gifts, favors, dollars, dick, and precious time out of men. We all have to respect the game from all angles. I use to wonder" how does a not so attractive guy bag a high level hot chick? "This brings us back to the point of women making their choices or decisions in a strategic manner, which in the end benefit them full circle. They have so many choices, that they can sit back and turn men away by the dozens and still have a large number to choose from. I have had women tell me that they have been horny as hell, meet a guy that says the right things, is "nice looking", and still opted to turn him down, settling for a night alone with the vibrator. This is done to hook the fish or to ensure that the fish is hooked, by speaking with him again the next week or so to see that he is still interested, and they move in for the kill. They see if he will put his money where he claims his heart is, and if he would verbally commit to them. The main goal is to hook the perfect fish that fits their vision of a happy comfortable lifestyle they dream about. That knight in shiny armor, tall, dark, and handsome sucker for love that is committed to a monogamous relationship is highly in demand. The female species understand, over stand, and plays this game as professionals.

These are some of the behaviors that I was taught to implement when dealing with women, and at an early age I became a fisherman. I started by first gathering the tools I needed for fishing. My tools were to be used when the fish bites and is in my net of seduction. At this point, you must possess tools and skills to keep them hooked.

These tools and skills were a broad vocabulary, through lots of reading, writing and conversations with people of all walks of life. Taking time to go to new places and see things to broaden horizons for myself. This helps us be able to hold a conversation about shit other than the things we learn running the streets or hanging with the fellas. Next, I had to converse with women to study how they respond, think and feel about certain issues and situations with the opposite sex.

This helped me to feel, relate and how to converse with women. It is important because it provided me with a clear vision and understanding of how to responds to any statement or response a woman makes to me. Conversations continue by adding older men to the list, preferable men who have pimp tendencies. Men who were obviously so called "lady killers" back in their day, they always say that it was due to their ability, to converse. These guys provided you with some of the wittiest responses that the younger generation has never heard. This is to separate me from other guys, the moment I open my mouth.

Next would be to make sure the bait is in place. I had to look at all of my features and sharpen them up as sharp as I could get them. This includes my skin, my smile, the walk, the clothes, the shoes and the scent. My hands, my hair and even the company I associated myself with, all these things need to be in place and top notch. After cleaning process, it was time to work on my associations. I made sure that the guys I hung around were hip to the game like myself and carried themselves accordingly. It does nothing for you to have lame "Squares" in your presence because women know" birds of a feather, flock together. As it also pertains to association, I had to connect with as many "girlfriends" that were very attractive, as I could.

I met several top notch women with no intent to score but to just associate with. I use my gifts to gab to start a cool relationship until the point they would be asking me to hang out sometimes. While hanging out, I keep my cool, drinking and socializing in the presence of other attractive women. There is nothing that can attract fine women, like fine women. This signifies to other fine women that you must be a "great catch" and this arouses their suspicion, to see exactly what these dime pieces saw in me. So you know I had my hooks ready.

When woman started to approach, the first thing that I did was put away my hooks. Now it was time to fish no matter how bad I wanted to make a move on them, I waited patiently. I was prepared to socialize for a little, let them know that it was very nice to meet them. Leave without asking for the number. This was a behavior that they were not familiar with, coming from the opposite sex. Its like the gazelle walking pass a lion, with the expectation to run, but the lion pay the gazelle no mind. Curiosity caused them to engage me to find out what drives this unusual behavior, and when they scratch the surface, it becomes more intriguing. Normally at this point, the hunter makes his move, but not this time. The conversation starts to become interesting and engaging to the ladies, only to end in an unusual manner. They are thinking, "He doesn't want my number," does he not think I'm attractive," what's going on"? If you continue this method, very few encounters like this will end without you getting their number, because they will offer it, or ask for your number. Regardless of which one it turns out to be, I win. What you have at this point gentleman, is a very attractive woman who is very interested.

Here is where it gets tricky, the day they call or the day you decided to call them. Being prepared to keep up the mystery is very important. It's time to put to use the word choice; the witty phrase that we learned from talking to older player's and pimps. The key is to say what they have never heard before in a way they have never heard it, or say what they have heard in a way they have never heard it.

This is important because it creates conversational impact that is needed to keep her "hooked." There is a missing piece that many guys don't have to go along with this impact, and it causes the dude to appear to be just like the rest. This missing piece is called the truth. What?

I know it sounds crazy but it is a proven fact that 65% to 70% of guys that are successful with getting what they want from females exactly the way they want it without hurting their feelings, tell the truth every time they are speaking to women. There are a large number of guys in this playing field that are compulsive liars, so that will separate you from them from the beginning. Simply tell the truth about your intentions, your situation, your likes and dislikes. Don't be afraid to add pieces of you to the equation because being you is done in the most natural manner. If you are looking for a monogamous relationship, a one night stand, an occasional "fuck buddy" or if you are not interested sexually at all, she will know where you stand. She has the choice to deal with it or pass on it, but either outcome, she will respect it. These are the words as they were revealed to me that I reveal to you.

SINGLE

Have you ever looked at the discovery channel when they were exploring the lion and how he lived? What are some things that you notice about the lion? What stands out? Depending on whom you ask, you might get some interesting behaviors. The first things, that stood out to me was his presence. His massive size, thick coat, large teeth and piercing stare in his eyes. This presence alone is intriguing to some, fearful to some, but respected by all. Like, the lion, the male species of human beings can in a since carry a similar affect. When the lioness gets one look at the lion, running freely throughout wild, hunting, and ruling, there is an un-denying attraction. When the man is single with demanding presence, freely moving about, there is an attraction to the female specious of humans. Since I was in the kindergarten, I can remember being complimented on my looks. At that point I didn't know what it meant or why girls behaved the way they did around me. I would get a sly glance, to a long stare, or a pretty smile to an unfortunate frown. I could even remember one girl that stuck her tongue out at me whenever I saw her. This was the beginning of the attraction girls had towards me, and the different ways they expressed it. I found myself getting different reactions, which spawn different relationships with each girl I encountered. Throughout my years up to puberty, these many relationships would be the beginning of promiscuity. I noticed that there were many things I liked about the ladies or should I just say females that presented themselves in many females that I've met. I like pretty faces, which could be a very broad characteristic due to the many types of pretty faces, from the many shades of complexion, race and nationality.

Then there are the small details in the face that can be very attractive on some women; but not as attractive on other women. I remember seeing a girl that was not pretty at all, but had eyes and lips that made her very sexy, to name an example.

There are attractive features found in every woman that makes it difficult to engage just one. There are also the physical features of the female that are present in all type of women and all type of ways. An example is nice breast, a nice ass, beautiful skin and nice hips. These blessing can and do fall on women of all walks of life and I was attracted. This is where it became interesting, what really drove me to the man I am, is that women of all walks of life were attracted to me; this made me develop a love and attraction towards being single. This is not to say all women liked me, because as we go on you will see what it's like to be single, and being me.

I was blessed with a huge heart. This huge heart truly has the ability to love strong and love many. I have room for so many different personalities, pretty faces and sexy physiques; conversation with women from all walks of life motivates me to engage in even more women. Its unquenchable thirst, because I always meet one more intriguing than next but not intriguing enough to sever ties with the previous one. There are things about each of them that are not present in all of them that I meet.

When I meet a girl, the first thing I look for is the connection. There has to be more than an attraction, because the ultimate ecstasy for me is a strong connection with a beautiful girl. There are many that are brought within arm's reach, however not embraced. I will touch more on these girls later, but for now, let's focus on the ones we embrace.

This takes us back to the Hunter, in which this is the school that I am going through and I am enjoying every moment of it at this time. I am on the prowl, however I am not aggressive. First of all, I take time and invest in my presence like clothes, shoes, cologne, and my business. Everything is on point from the outside to the inside, hygiene, health, physique, skin, etc. This is very important because as I stated earlier, I'm only into those who are into me. If this is the case, you want to ensure those that choose you, are of a good selection. I wanted the cream of the crop without having to chase them. I came to realize that getting the finest girl in the school often came with stipulations I did not want to give in to.

Some of the guys you see with the hottest girls jump through hoops you wouldn't believe. I didn't want them at that expense. I do recall the period of my life in which I had not reached this understanding, that involve nice looking girls, but a lot of headaches, issues, lies, and explaining. I would tell them anything they wanted to hear or become who they wanted me to be, just for the luxury of sex and occasional "trophy show." This is when I'm out in the public for others to see her and possibly judge or solidify me as being on a certain level. When the guys are at this point, there are many lies that are told, and lies are like a scent that follows you around. It follows you around because every time you tell one, and forget about it, there's always someone who remembers.

The more you tell, the more you stink. Lies are a sign of fear, and immaturity that plagues human beings. Fear of being who you are as a person or fear of revealing the way you are and feel. After a lie is told, I would feel as if I had really accomplished something, the goal of guiding the perception of people I come in contact with. This accomplishment started to mean less to me the more times I succeed and it became tiring. It became the exercise that you continue to do in which there are not healthy results. However we are faithful to this exercise for the short-term satisfaction. The pussy was good at this time, but believe me it could have been much better. I could have had not only the satisfaction of being with a hot girl, doing things I fantasized about for pleasure, as well as the true feeling and understanding that this hot girl was actually fucking me. Pay close attention to what I'm about to say: if I was becoming who they wanted me to be, for a moment of their precious time, then at that very moment, I am not being me. When the time of intimacy happens it's not with me, but the perception of me that I purposely attempted to cast.

That's what lying does in my opinion. Many guys could care less about focusing on this truth due to being so occupied with focusing on what they wanted to get out of the encounter. This is what separated me from them at an early age. I wanted to be involved with women that adored me when I was on point or slightly slipping, because it's called being real. If the time came that I had to lose some of the things I have or have to take step back to get ahead, the women in my life were more supportive than the average woman would be.

It's because I casted a truthful reflection of my life, my wisdom and experiences. I did not cast the image of the perfect man. Many of us make this mistake initially, and when it turns out to be untrue, they will separate themselves from you. I came to realize that being me wasn't all that bad. There was nothing to be ashamed of, just a uniqueness that can't be found in any other person on the face of the planet. This was something that I cherish, and comfortably display every day of my life. This confidence started to shine through whatever situation I was in and attracted many women. It also revealed to me a differentiated mind state or level I was on than the average guy. I would observe how guys I know would handle situations and responded to behaviors and actions of women. It amused me to see how we can appear to have it all figured out yet be on a page in the chapter of the book, I have read several years back. They spend so much time and place the most emphasis on the outside as opposed to the inside. The spirit, the soul, and mind is what I really wanted to devote time to in the words of the legendary rap artist, Willie "D" of the legendary group, The Geto Boys", conversation ruled the nation. A wise man told me once that the ability to hold charming and engaging conversations with women is the key to be able to have your choice of beautiful women. I'm not crazy, but that wise man is me. I have conversation of self-realizations often with myself.

The ability to respond will get you anywhere you desire to be. When I was 13, there was a girl so attractive that came to our neighborhood to work at the community center. Of course there were several hunters that were interested. She was 16 years old and far more advanced at least that's what I thought. She would go through her workday fighting off sexual advances by the dozen and I would just observe. Now, I didn't think for one second that she was innocent of lust or sexual experiences, it just seem as if every boy tried to engage her the exact same way.

There was the occasional whistling at her, complimenting her, calling her name and asking for her phone number, to aggressively grabbing her arm or touching her on her butt. I on the contrary did none of the above, just observed. One day she notice how she had advancement issues with every young man except myself, and out of curiosity she wanted to know why. So the day she saw me she asked me my name and told me that I was cute. Now I am in shock but I am composed, so I responded in a way that she did not expect. She expected the occasional blush and for me to say" thank you and I think you are cute too." This was a feeble attempt to feel me out or to engage me to the point of acting just like the other boys. I saw that when she was dealing with or fighting guys off with a stick and turning them down was amusing to her. It was keeping her going, feeding her vanity. After she gave me the compliment, I looked at her without a smile and said" cute? Sweetheart, Puppies are cute" and she looked at me and did not know how to respond. It was not disrespectful, but it was I encouraging her to choose another adjective. From that point on she wanted to talk to me just to see what I would say next. This was an example of the ability to respond.

All throughout my life, the ability to respond kept me on the minds of many women. It has made one night stands happen with girls in cities that I have lived or visited for the weekend. This gift at one point in my life became a curse as well, due to it made it difficult to get in with girls and move on. Being such a likeable guy makes it difficult to play, due to on the receiving end of it all there are feelings. Sometimes feelings got in the way of me getting what I came for or after I got what I came for, gets in the way of me and the young lady just being friends. Yes, sometime they wanted more. Wanting more made them not want to give up their bodies so soon, in the attempt to keep me; these girls felt that if they wanted to give it to me this fast, many other girls have given it up this fast.

So they try and differentiate themselves from the rest by holding out on the first date. Hoping it grows into more and possibly maintains my respect. This didn't work on a man like myself because if she didn't give in tonight, it will be another girl tonight, and then another the next night until the new girl finally comes around. When little Ms. Self-Respect decides she's ready to serve me, then it happens. No respect loss, none maintained, no respect gained.

Respect is a clear understanding that is earned from a confident individual that displays this confidence in a non-compromising way. There have been all, if not many women that have gained my respect.

Being single, I run across different characteristics that I respect from women from how they expect to be treated to whom and what they wish to be. One thing that really put me on fast track to respecting a woman was honesty.

A woman that was true to who she is and had an uncompromising way of living. Respect is a word I hear consistently on the single track but it is requested or demanded more than it is earned. I've met girls, who carried hoops around in their purse, and the moment a guy said hello, they were out and she was expecting him to jump through them. This approach is the very reason women like this do not have the respect of a man. Some men will jump through those hoops long enough to appear to be what she is looking for or gives her the impression that she has him "trained", until she gives him some pussy. At this point, as it pertains to the hoops, he is a little slower to jump through them. When she "barks" out a request, he doesn't grant it as fast as he used to. Now she feels like 'I thought he love me, respected me", but actually, he respected what he needed to do to get the sex.

Many women have been on this side of the spectrum and gradually picked up and move in to a new encounter, focused on not letting this happen again. Some however become bitter from the experience, while others learn and gain more of an understanding of respect. Then there are the women who feel this was a one-time mistake, use the same method assuming it will not happen again. They become paranoid, watching every move, facial expressions and listening to every word the next guy says. They are the women that are quick to over react assuming the worst or that they are on to the game he is playing.

This can ultimately keep a young beautiful single lady, frustrated, and single. Bitter and feeling that "there are no good men out there." This is when I enter the scene, a different man, cut from a different cloth, the truth. This is how I gain my respect.

It starts with being appealing to the eye of women, basically having you together mentally, physically, and spiritually. Being totally confidant in who you are. Not ashamed of where you are in your life, and focused on where you are going. I have a plan, something that I want to achieve at least every year of my life.

This plan also involve me evolving as a person broadening my horizons, which includes traveling every chance that I get, trying new foods, and holding casual conversation with strangers. Reading as many books as you can and watching documentaries that make you aware of things you didn't know. I turn my flaws and weaknesses into possibilities to one day become some of my strength.

Last but certainly not lease, I tell the truth. Verbalizing how you feel was an important piece that helps me build a connection with women I have met. If there wasn't a connection felt, I didn't deal with the girl, just held casual conversation and went on my way. She then became one of the friendly strangers that I conversed with and moved on. Never being proactive in asking for the number, but allowing her to offer her number or ask for your number. Women truly respect patience in a man and understanding of where you and she stand with each other. This brings on a level of comfort, which brings on her being willing to let go and express herself around me without feeling embarrassed or worried about how you will feel about her. She will open up because she sees that you will open up. This connection leads to any and everything you want to know about a woman, as well as exploring every inch of her sexuality, all without a commitment of monogamy, but with a commitment to be true and to tell her the truth.

When this connection is built, I would cherish every moment of her, making our time together unforgettable but to a certain extent "Limited". Now, listen closely because her comes a curve ball. I said make the experience unforgettable yet limited. This means always say what you mean and mean what you say. When I meet and connect with some women they are truly remarkable individuals and they can be infectious.

They can reel you in with kindness, wittiness, intelligence, beauty, and they can reel you in sexually. This is the point where if you are not careful you may play a card that throws a monkey wrench as they call it, in your whole situation. I have found myself getting too attached to her, until the point where our understanding of our situation becomes a grey area. She treated me so well that it could make a player slip up one night and either use the L-word or the"I think we need to see each other more often". Trying to limit our time together, I would sometimes advise her that we cannot hang out this weekend because I was busy when I was indeed sitting at home. I didn't want to over expose myself to her and give her time to miss me.

The connection can be so good and so strong, another slip up can be, when you call to see what she has going on tonight and you hear a guy in the background while she says," tonight is not a good night". What do you do? That feeling starts to creep into you where you feel a little bit of jealousy. This is what drives certain guys toward what we call **"Jumping out of the window"**, asking to be exclusive, getting into the exact situation we didn't want to be in.

This marks the point in which the single days began to approach the end. Notice, I said begin to approach because the end of the single life is nowhere near at this time. What happens is the young lady will sometimes feel swept off her feet, and fall right into your arms until one day, you wake up thinking," what the hell have I done." What you have done was take the very situation we have eluded for years and embraced it to try and keep a young lady exclusively to ourselves. Once this happens or this feeling hits you, we go back to the man that we were realizing that, as I like to say, "We jump a dime to get to a nickel."

We then slide back into our normal way of being, single and ready to date whoever we like. But now the situation has slightly changed.

We have lured the young lady into the promise of a monogamous relationship, only to realize it's not what we want. So, now here comes the lying, due to us not wanting to hurt feelings, or come clean about it being our fault the monogamous situation occurred. Another way it could probably turn would be if the young lady rejects your offer of exclusiveness, which sends you between the legs and arms of one of your other women. Squeezing her tight and cherishing the relationship you have with her, thinking how happy you are that she is available to fill the sudden void due to rejection. This could possible lead to the young lady who was there for us, to start feeling as if she had finally won you over and a closer relationship has begun.

This is what happen when a player fall off the wagon. It has happen to me before and I'm not ashamed to admit it, but I pick up my pride, lick my wounds, and put my feelings back in check, or back in my pocket.

The lion is freely roaming the jungle again after this point and back to his old self. He takes this as a lesson learned as well as something he can educate other brothers on. When the lion gains his swagger back, the female can sense it and they continue admiring and sometimes lusting after him. He allows the fish to bite and live his life. He adds more names to his black book and continues to pop open boxes of condoms.

The fact that I am single also allows unlimited time for me to focus on my career. I spend massive amount of time trying to climb the corporate ladder, or sharpening my skills to be the best I can be professionally. Some of the most powerful individuals in life and in business are not seriously involved with anyone or tied down by family. Don't get me wrong; family is important to me, but being able to provide for that family is the most important thing to me.

I did not want to be the young guy who has a family early, and is hindered from being all he can be, and in places he needs to be at the time he needs to be there. Success has always been about focus, persistence, and timing. So the single life was best for this young lion in the wild. This is not to say success can't happen to the family man but to say that with family, you have to redefine what success mean to "you", meaning your entire family rather than what success is and its meaning to "you", yourself.

When a lion is at his point of being free of responsibilities other than himself, working and taking responsibility only for him, this period, can be looked at as selfish, or as women would say, "Immature" stage. I hear women talk about men some ways I thought I understood but didn't, when they referred to certain guys as childish or immature.

I do know that some of us are at the age of putting away our childish things, changing our childish thoughts, letting go of mama's hand and being a lion. I didn't believe how some single guys were acting, giving the women a right to call it how it truly is. But some of us are considered immature when we are over the age of 25 and not looking to settle down, shack up, or settle in a monogamous relationship. We still want to run the jungle freely, seeing or sexing whom we choose. However, I don't see this as immature behavior. As long as a man is taken care of his own, those closest and dear to him, and is very respectful of others, displaying gentleman qualities, he is not immature if he does not want to be exclusive with anyone.

After years of being a lion that I am, approaching adulthood, I found myself having what I thought were deeper feelings that I have had for a young lady. Every activity I was involved in, friends I hung out with, I found myself calling her when I was done. When I settled in for the night, it was done with her. I didn't have a car back in those days, so every opportunity I had that gave me access to a car, I wanted to go and see her.

This was also the period where I began to have sex on a consistent basis with a certain special someone. This is the period of the girlfriend. I actually had a girlfriend, whom to her, I was her only one and she would have like to believe that she was my only one. The thought of her feeling that we were exclusive, brought such a happy feeling that I did what I could in order to keep it that way. I was not exclusive to her but I was not going to tell her.

Her smile was truly important to me and the way she made me feel kept me around. She was beautiful, and I was a young fool. As a kid, I have an excuse for my ignorance, allowing myself to live this lie on behalf of someone else happiness, and my selfishness. However as an adult there is not excuse. Being single, there comes a time when you are together but not engaged, or haven't entertained the thought of marrying this someone, but we continue to live life together, going out, having fun, spending the night with each other, looking out for each other's well-being.

We as guys ignorantly think that things will go on the same way without her someday asking about your feelings towards marriage or settling down. We know it's coming, but we don't "keep it real" from the point of us realizing what we have with this young lady, we get caught up in the jealousy, and arguing about being faithful. Arguing when she sometimes don't act like she has a man. All the while me and this young lady stick together and make whatever we have worked.

This is included under the single chapter due to regardless of what you believe, at this time you are still single. We have to understand, that where ever you are in your life, or whatever level you are on, it's all about one thing. Where are you going, where is it going. The situation, what's the next step? Sometimes we forget that the only thing that is certain in life is change. What happens next? We as single guys in this situation love to try and stop the hands of time, the inevitability of change from happening right about this point. It's selfish but we are known to try and hold a woman at this point. Put her life on hold and not want anything different, until we are ready for something different.

When the day comes that she wants to talk about evolving we are known to do 1 of 3 things **(A) push it off, changing the subject. (B) Get upset about her forcing us to change the good thing that we do have or (C) pacify her, by talking about it and make false steps towards the change, until finally one day you are standing at the altar.** Option C is done strictly out of fear of losing her to this comfortable environment that you have created. Out of these 2 reactions, neither has a favorable long-term impact on this relationship. We forget the power of honesty without fear.

Giving an honest explanation as to why you feel how you feel will only lead to the best thing. Sometimes it's sweet to the mouth but bitter to the belly, but it's better for both individual and will lead to a mutual respect for each other. Honesty without fear is the route to take in this situation, in which single people should not be afraid to take, but often are. This is the ideal time to be honest, because there are no legal ties. There is no property to divide up; you are not at the point where you are totally dependent on each other, so a break up might be not only emotionally but also financially devastating at this time. Often times there are no kids involved at this point. These are several reasons for us not to fear honesty; however we do at this point. When I was at this point, I feared hurting the other person now, but substituted it for totally devastating her emotionally, financially in the future. It was idiotic but I didn't have anyone to give it to me this vivid at that point. It's even more devastating because now the young lady feels that you had the chance to be a man and be honest, but you chickened out. There is another area of being a single guy that many of us are at or have returned to. It's the guy that enjoys the freedom of being single and he attempts to exploit it every chance he gets. There is the level of deceit that is encountered as well as us truly not caring to understand the feelings of the opposite sex others. There is promiscuity to the maximum, due to us still in this school of the hunter.

It's the uncontrollable pursuit towards sex by any means that guide the thinking of these individuals, and is a danger to good girls all over the world. These are the heart breakers that young girls or wives tell you about that truly impacted their life. This single guy is only a small percentage of the players that are out lurking in the public, but not every player. These players give the true players a bad name. It is the reason that women started referring to all guys as dogs or all players at least. But being a player is not what you think ladies. I will share with you the true meaning of a player, what they look like, and how they could be a positive impact to your life.

I must start at advising you what a player isn't before explaining what a true player is. We must explore your perception as well as the perception gained by women in order to break it all down and build it up accurately.

The brother with no regard for what a ladies likes, wants or needs, his only concern is the number of girls he has tackled throughout his life. He keeps a tally of all that have fell victim to his charm, good looks, and lies, with the intentions of self-pleasure as well as reveling in his so called success. He used every aspect of his being to lure in, manipulate and humiliate innocent curious minds for the thrill of an orgasm.

He is solely about himself and flees at any sign of responsibility, and womanizes his way through life. The heartbreaker, who will lay up with any girl that is willing or any girl that is unwilling whom he could knowingly convince. This is very ugly monster that I have just painted a picture of, but please don't be afraid. This boogie monster in this form is about as real as the one hiding in your closet when you were a little girl. These are true characteristics of a player, but keep in mind that players have many more characteristics that I did not list, and they are not as scary. The truth is the monster I described is really attributes of many guys in the world spread out thin amongst a host of others.

You may have encountered one of your last boyfriends, who were as nice as he could be but possesses one of the characteristic of the boogie monster painting. Some are honestly closer to the boogie monster painting than others and look awfully like him, but not exactly like him. The ones that are closes to fitting the description (ladies, this may shock you) are not true players at all. They are what we refer to as extremist or pretenders. They are the ones who take all of the things (stereotypical) that a player should be, and they try to be it to the 10th power. There is nothing natural about the way these character are unless they have pretended so long as they say, "The mask of the actor is prone to become his face". These individual are the ones that are disagreeing with me as I speak, but the way you feel is just that and I truly respect it.

Walk with me as I describe what true player is and how they can impact your life in good ways ladies. To start, the true player looked similar or had some physical features identical to the Boogie Monster Painting; however this was the case in his younger days. I believe a true player must know what a true player is not, in order to be a true player.

He has graduated from the school of the hunter and became a fisherman. I will list some more characters that you may have never heard associated with a True Player but they are. They are as follows; Patient, Respectful, Charming, Educated, Caring, Hardworking, Optimistic; sensitive; attractive; a wordsmith processing the gift to gab; an individual; confident; healthy; a teacher; a student; honest; goal oriented; he listens to the fools and to the experts in life. I'm sure after viewing the list you may come up with even more. But the picture I've just painted is a tricky picture.

It sounds like your dream man, but remember, these are characteristics and not personalities. Characteristics describe how you are; your personality guides these characteristics to be displayed in a manner that shapes your values in life. In a nutshell, possessing all of these listed characteristics sounds like a true dream man, but the personality of this dream man can fuck it all up.

Now, for an important piece to the puzzle, how can this True player impact your life? Ladies, looking at this list it may be self-explanatory to some but I will still give it to you as clear and concise as I can. I will explain how dealing with a True player can be different than you may think and leave no room for misunderstandings, which is the soul reasons for heartbreaks, confusion, which is prevalent in many relationships. This leads to disconnects, frustrations, and possibly domestic violence. A true player lets you know exactly where they stand, and you will know the person you are dealing with. He stands right between truth and real life, so there is no room for misunderstanding. You must respect an individual who let you know clearly where they stand, even if they are wrong.

He is charming and very respectful of the women he deals with, and being with him, there is no need to expect anything less. He is intelligent and a true people person, because he can walk into any room with any people and gently fit right in, never degrading himself or being who he is not. Mothers, Grandmothers, Aunts, and other family member will love him because he has the gift that shine through that all women can identify.

All women have a natural instinct to get a man. These skills could range anywhere from below standard to advanced, which of course makes some women more effective than others. It normally starts from her strongest attribute or as some like to call, their strongest assets.

Being with a true player helps women identify theses asset, the ones that are blatant or obvious about her, in a way that is so effective that they attract men, good men they would have otherwise not been interested or interested in the obvious. **Example:** When you have a nice ass, it's difficult to not attract men that are focused on what they want to do to your nice ass. When this happens, a women's natural instinct is **(A) to see this as a turn off due to it may indicates this is the only reason, he is interested, or (B) use the attraction he has for your ass to get what wants from him.** Even if it is that he is attractive, has money or whatever. A true player would teach you to highlight an attribute that he is not focused on in a way that is effective, and teach her how to fish for exactly what she wants from this guy. The guy at that point will take notice and continue to follow suit or he would opt to try elsewhere either way she would have not ran off a potentially good man, or wasted her time and body on one not worthy. One of the most important aspect about benefiting from a true player is transparency, which dispels any rumors; suspicious feelings; hurt; disgruntles, violence and hard break ups.

Women place lots of emphasis on a "good man" as one who is truthful. Horror stories that women have about men they have dated ends 90% of the time with the guy being a liar. If we changed the way we were, in the ways of a true player, and not just a guy that's playing, we could fix close to 90% of the problems between a man and woman. Women are also guilty of being players/true players. This will be touched on shortly.

A true player is well versed in the English language, knows how to verbalize how he feels and does so elegantly. He is one who, every chance he gets picks up knowledge, or is eager to learn something new. This mentality alone helps women benefit from being with a true player. No matter what level a woman is on in her life, she is always intrigued by someone who can stimulate her mind.

If you can introduce a woman to something new and beneficial to her in a clean-cut neat package, she will be attracted. Mind stimulation is more important than the physical aspect of sex, because the physical aspect of sex is useless without the mental. A true player is educated about himself and his unlimited potential to go anywhere he wants and become what he wishes to see himself as. It's not just about getting a degree. When a true player stimulates a woman's mind it becomes an engaging joyful, eager to learn challenge to be around him. This challenging environment that a true player sets for women helps them strive for and rise to the occasion of all aspects of her life. Simply put, if you hang around positive and successful you will be positive and successful.

Another aspect of a woman's life that benefits from being with a true player is sexually. The aspect that many of you have been waiting to hear about is, what about "physical pleasure?" If a woman's mind is stimulated, the individual that does the stimulating actually has the means of taking her where ever he wants her to go sexually.

He can bring you up and he can bring you down, left, right. A true player uses his powers for the good so you don't have to worry, you are in good hands. 80% to 85% of sex, I mean great sex is the mental. If a woman is not mentally into you then she is less likely to reach climax or level of ecstasy she is capable of. The fake player relies on the physical and allows the physical to please a woman, and wonder why he does not get the reaction from her he desires. Most women understand but many will soon mature to over stand that a big dick and an attractive body on a man is not the full package. Sexually, I have had women tell me that they are used to these pretty boys that works out every week, 6 pack and all, and how it was still something missing. What was missing was the focus, time, and energy of these guys was spent on how they look on the outside.

Little time was spent building up the muscle between their 2 ears. They feel that, "the sexier I look, the more women I will bag." Don't get me wrong, to a certain extent they are right, we are mostly physical beings caught up in the physical on this planet. Many women are roped in at the site of what they can consider a "fine man". But what's next when they don't fully deliver? Women are back out in the field or jungle, exploring their options looking for another "lion". A true player that stimulates a woman's mind spiritually, professionally, educationally, has a greater impact on women if he can stimulate her mind sexually. He can use his word choice, demeanor, and delivery to surround her in what she sees as a comfortable environment.

This comforting environment allows a woman to be themselves with no worries of the man she is with at the time, not understanding, getting the wrong idea, or judging her.

She feels good in the presence of a true player, or at the moment she hears his voice, on the phone.

A true player learns that when he can provide or create an environment that is comfortable to a woman, you experience her true self. I have had intimate conversation with women on the phone that would have them masturbate at the mere thought of me being in their presence. These are women that I have yet to have intercourse with, on the phone being verbally taking to a level of sexual bliss, masturbating and climaxing. The true player at this point has her aroused, engaged, and anticipating the first time. When that first time comes, there are no expectation due to the fact that the true player makes her climax without touching her, so bringing her to climax while touching her make it happen much faster and much more intense. This is the time where the true player delivers giving her a night she will never forget that started with him stimulating her mind in other ways. Ladies, this is the definition of great sex. Being stimulated mentally and physically, simultaneously driven towards ecstasy.

The true player can benefit your young life in many ways that I have spoken about and many ways I have not, due to some of the ways being personal to you. With all the pro's to being with a true player, the one

Con that stands out is the fact that, besides being open, honest, caring, charming, smart and fun, the one thing he will not be is your only one. This is the part that will make a man/woman overlook the wonderful experience. But the true player is there to get you prepared to meet your one true love. He helps you understand what to expect dealing with a man and what not to accept. He gives you the motivation that you need to climb the ladder in whatever career you choose, due to you not focusing on "when am I going to find my one true love", at such a young age. This is a distraction in young women all over the world. This deter them from reaching the heights they are capable of potentially and tie herself down chasing what all women want at some part of their lives. To hold, obtain, and own their vision of happiness exactly the way she visualized it. There are certain situations, things and people you will come across in your life that will be perfect, but throughout a woman's life, she can't seem to understand that this vision of happiness cannot be obtained because happiness is a pursuit towards satisfying a state of mind. It's a never-ending pursuit, due to the mind constantly striving for what's in front of it. After what's in front of it becomes what she already have, it is replaced by something else. So when she tries to find her very own monogamous relationship in her twenties and even her early to mid-thirties, she finds a part of her happiness. She now starts on a journey to shaping and molding that situation with the man she is with into what she wants. Women are sometimes inconsiderate of the man they have chosen and try to align who he is with their ideal mate or their ideal mate's characteristics and behaviors.

Sometimes this works out well, and they go on to become a happy union. Many guys, who conform to this vision of their women to make her happy, later start to drift in the direction that makes them happy. This is almost always not what the woman wants and it takes a turn for the worst. Sometimes after she meets the guy and begins to attempt to align him with what she wants, the guy realizes it and the relationship falls apart, resulting to them moving on to new situation. The expectation, or should I say unrealistic expectation, of what a lot of women have of men have caused them to be single and searching. But a true player prepares them by giving them realistic outlook on her expectations so that she is better equipped to move on from him to a man that will be supportive of her realistic expectations. These are benefits of dealing with a true player.

Single women go through different stages in their life that men need to understand, to keep harmony between the genders. When a man meets a woman, he is at a certain stage in his life, and she is at a certain stage. If they both were able to identify the stages they are at the moment of them getting to know each other, it would allow them to make clear headed decision on the expectations of their encounter, and if it will be brief or ongoing. This saves them time, heartbreak and misconception. These stages of the woman are very similar to these of the man.

You have the fisher lady. The difference is that women are fisher for the most part of their lives, only switching from it during parts of their lives they feel it is truly necessary. Women are raised to be discreet due to the fact that scientifically they think with both sides of their brain. This helps with reasoning and weighing out options.

They are raised to choose a man from the ones who approach them or show interest due to the fact that men are raised to be the hunters, to approach and show interest. Men always go after the woman during this stage. The single woman, depending on where she is on the age ladder will fluctuate to different stages she feels is necessary. But overall, they will do what they have to do to obtain the vision of their happiness exactly the way the visualize it. Ultimately the majority of women want a mate that will be theirs and only theirs. Women want a man that they can call their own as well as a mate that feels the same way about them. They also want the full package, a great personality; great sex life; a sensitive individual that can and will express himself verbally, handsome; nice built body structure; financially able, etc. This doesn't seem like much to ask for in a vision overall, but what causes frustration is when they are not simultaneously present in the guys they meet. So naturally they go for what's important to them at this point in their lives. Going back to the age ladder, this is why it is important, but it does not always tell a woman's story accurately. You have to weigh out every aspect, including actually listening to what's she tells you.

Things that she says and how she says them will help identify the level she is on. Most important you as the man must be open and honest in telling her about yourself because "an open mind and heart will open a mind and a heart." She will open up to you and the real will come out.

Women can also be like hunters, focused on pleasing themselves with one of the favorable aspect of a man. It could be from his nice looks to his charming personality to his financial or celebrity status, etc. But after being raised to focus on one aspect or being frustrated with not being able to find all characteristics in one man, this is a route some of them take.

This could make her seem heartless at times, direct or uninterested in you, but the key thing to understand that it's not about you at all. It's about her experience in attempting to get what she wants in her vision of happiness. This is where we find the so-called gold-digger, nymphomaniac's freaks, shallow superficial ladies, etc. These are the extreme personalities and are a part of the stage of the hunter. Now they fluctuate within this stage switching their focus and interest to whatever is important to them at that time. Men must realize once again that it is not about you but about what this specific man that they like can bring to their BIG PICTURE. Everything is beautiful as long as you are who she wants you to be and the way she wants you to be, then things would appear to be ok. Some guys feel that it is their duty to be pleasing to his woman due to an addictions to seeing her happy.

They also want to see her happy so that another man won't cross her mind due to us providing exactly what she wants and needs. But men slowly start to drift towards things that are pleasing to them, after so much time aligning our behaviors with what our women, or woman in general feels is favorable.

Men start to focus a little more on pleasing themselves with things that entertain them. Now these things that entertain the guy are not explored as much when the main focus is centered on his strong attraction toward the woman, he puts that on the "backburner" and focus solely on her; what she likes. This creates an expectations going forward that they can't keep up with all of the relationship. When the focus shift her slightly from what she became accustomed to, she does whatever she cans to get it back. She will do whatever she can to get more of what was happening to happen again. The famous "we need to talk" conversations, she will complain, argue, or even leave you. It may start with threats, but it's all done in order to get you to be what you were or "act right" as some woman like to call it. It is a scientific fact that woman overall, think with both sides of their brain and we only think with one side. What does that mean? It means that she has the power, and she uses it to benefit her, totally thinking things through and analyzing things important to her from all angles.

Notice, I didn't say" all things" but only things relevant and important to her. We all know what is important to a woman, is happiness. Each woman has her own pick of what that is, but it encompasses the same things; Career success, financial stability, happy healthy family, happy relationship. Women are a simple species, just like men, but woman have a more complex view on getting these happy aspects of their lives. You can sit and talk to these women and get their different viewpoints on being happy, that many seem complex, but their viewpoints will include the four aspects. Some guys will be more opt to make this date the last date for women with detailed and complex views and expectations. They will go for the women that want to have fun and know how to express it in a simple manner. The women that leave, the women who know exactly what they want will be left wondering, "are there any good men in my city?" Where are they?' The answer to that question is, they are out with the women who express having fun on the first dates more so than the ones who discuss the expectations they have.

I know we like to ask personal questions about you, and that you are being honest due to not wanting to mislead the guy or waste your time on someone who clearly does not want what you want. Waist time with a guy you may be willing to give to but he is not willing to give what you want at this time. Women do not understand that they must take a more subtle approach. Position having a good time with the guy on the first few dates, but not to the point where you are doing things you are not comfortable with. This is very important. Fun is major part of a relationship that must be visible when he sees you or think of you. If we can't have fun with each other, then the relationship will fail. Spread your list of expectation out the first few months you are associated with him. Stand strong on your values; you don't have to always verbalize them to let him know they are important to you. Also be open to dating others during this period. When you first start dating a guy, there is nothing that will shake him up, like knowing that the female he just started dating is and will continue to date other guys. This is important because we feel the same way.

He has his little black books filled with potentials before he met you and I know you don't think that after the first couple of dates with you that he has burned the black book. He has not called up all his "friends" that he is intimate with or hoping to be intimate with and said, "Hey, I'm currently dating someone new that I think is special, so I want be calling or seeing you anymore." This is not real, so it is important for you as women not to approach dating the new guy like this, women don't call up all of their potentials and say that either. So why do they go into dating looking to "catch a good one," rather than just to meet a friend and let things happen as they may? Some women like to use time, thinking they are not getting any younger, but we should not be confined by space and time.

Anything you make happen, that does not naturally happen, you will have to make it last. Making this happen is what we settle for other than understanding that fun things happen to fun people. You will stay in the mist of prosperous, fun, people doing fun things to balance out our stressful lives. Women of today are so frustrated with their sex life or romantic side; they lean hard in their careers. They become power players in their careers and it is difficult for her to turn that demeanor off when going out to have a good time. Men are only intimidated by successful women who wear their success in their professional life out at night in their personal life.

This makes a guy feel like she is out of his league or just plan not the type of chic he is interested in. It can be a turn off yet the ladies, who are like this, can't seem to put 2 and 2 together to see that this hinders their ability to meet men and just have fun. Some women feel that it is a good defense mechanism to push away guys who may have intentions that are less than what she expects at this point in her mature life. This is true as well, however people are at different stages in life and just because a guy is intimidated today doesn't mean they can't step up and be the man you really need to satisfy your relationship needs.

When a girl does allow a guy in that may have failed her first impression test, due to her never realizing how she approaches the relationship, she never changes. She never stepped out of her corporate role because she feels this approach has helped her gain everything successful in her life, including now, a new man. This approach does start to become tiring to the guy and when he wants to have fun, he thinks about the girls he used to have fun with or the girls he may see in his everyday life. This makes him really want a break from his new chic. The uptight chic that knows what she wants and knows how to get it makes the relationship a living boot camp, and drives guys out into the strip clubs and bars.

That's why we call our rendezvous with the other girls our "get away", because we want to get away. This is why they are called our "jump offs", because we can jump on and jump off without the stress your main lady gives you. We ask women can they get away, and when you come to the get away with a hard-core business demeanor with up front expectations, they wonder why guys try their best to get away from you.

MARRIED

It is considered to be the best way of showing someone you truly love him or her. Spiritually and legally attaching yourself to another in what is commonly known as "Holy Matrimony" is the ultimate way to show that you are in love with someone, and is considered the natural progression of a relationship. For many this happens but only for some it last forever. First comes the meeting, the dating, the connection, the love, the care; the engagement, the dress, the rings, and the wedding. It is a beautiful thing to see two people say vows before God to commit to each other till death and to work out any issues together. To bring children into the world in a caring and loving environment creating a family that breads more possible productive people in society. The time that they go through happy, sad, joy and pain are only obstacles, which once weathered, should only make us stronger and love each other even more. Putting the kids through school, watching them grow into successful young adults who will one day create their own families hopefully in the image and often the likeness of mom and dad. Growing old and grey together with your spouse of several decades living out our last days in peace until we are both resting in peace.

This is the picture that many strive for hoping to paint, but as they say my picture can't be your picture, and no one's pictures can be picture perfect. So we must deal with the flaws and different situations that make up your picture, taking the happy and the sad, the joy and the pain together, hoping to balance or tip the scale as best we can towards getting this picture. This picture has become the stage or stakes that are set and measured as being a successful story that we all would like to have but many of us won't have. One day we must all decided that when it comes to this picture, it does not define me or my family. We have to say, "fuck" that picture and anyone who feels I am not successful without it, and paint our own.

Those who are liberated from concerns about how they look or how they appear to others in society are the people that reach happiness. These people are more likely to understand that you have to define happiness for yourself, and not let society or others tell us what it is. We often pursuit happiness before defining what it means to us. There are many who buy big expensive cars, buy the big house and they marry the prettiest girl because of the fact that they feel this is happiness or success. It makes you feel great that when people see how you are living that they say to themselves" man, they really have it going on" or they are balling". This is what we like to feel, that everyone else feels about us. Some want to be envied. One of the common mistakes made is to marry the prettiest girl. We were raised to find a wife; get married and start a family. We looked at this as being traditionally the thing to do but we never questions is it the thing to do that is right for me?" Men assume it is because of how it would make them look or they feel that if you don't wed the one that makes you feel special or seem right for you, then you will miss out, grow old and be alone. Extreme, but this is how many of us think. Sometimes we feel this way about a young lady, but try to hold off popping the questions as long as we can because deep down we know it's not our time. Then here comes the fork in the road that is set by our significant others call the ultimatum, either we get married or we need to go our separate ways.

One of three things happen after this conversation,

(a) We decide that, it's not the time and end the relationship.
(b) We make the ever so popular promise that it will happen soon, to buy us more time to the next time this comes up.
(c) We take the leap, buy the ring, and set the date.

Let's talk about **(B)** first. This is the most popular choice that is made due to the fear of commitment and an equal fear of losing the individual. We as humans string the significant other along until we finally make the decision to surrender. What we fail to realize is that the longer you string that person along, the more you become the person they want you to be. This is why those who choose option **(B)**, a high percentage of these automatically fall into option **(C)**. We really believe happiness with a significant other comes along only once and that if you find it (or think you found it), we need to do whatever to keep that person. This is an example of becoming who that person wants you to be because of what you believe. This promise that we make turns out to be the conversation we try to avoid all the way up until an ultimatum is made. "Commit to me or find yourself someone else." Marry me or I am leaving." We do what we can to pacify the individual to keep from talking about it. The fear is so strong we mistake it as being love. We make the decision to move to option **(C)** out of fear of losing that someone, or being without that someone, thinking, that it is truly love. Just because you can't bear the thought of seeing that special someone with someone else, we make the rash decision to jump.

After you jump, where do you land? We land in an ongoing struggle to do exactly what option **(B)** and **(C)** was designed to do, keep someone else happy. To keep your significant other happy is why we promise that we will give them what they want to push off the issue to keep them happy, or we make the decision to surrender, just to make them happy. I call it surrender because over **95%** of married men would be happy as girlfriend and boyfriend.

Plus an alarming 40% to 50% of women would be happy in the same predicament. The question is why? I will explain. We as human being get so attached or caught up emotionally that we are blinded or blind ourselves to the stages you identify that your mate is currently on. We know the truth but refuse to acknowledge or we see the signs and choose to ignore that your mate is still in the stage of the hunter. We feel that we will wait it out and deal with what comes. We know that at some point in everybody's life, change happens and we can only see that day, in tunnel vision. What's sad as well is that sometimes our mates get the courage to identify and acknowledge that you are not ready, and some of us go so far as to deny it to prove them wrong. We actually deny it because they are afraid to lose this person.

This in turn will make the person who identifies this, overlook the signs or falsely believe that the person is ready because we truly want our partners to be ready when we are. When we opt for option (**C**), the surrender, this is where it becomes interesting. We go in the union with hopes of growing old and gray together only to realize after a while that you are actually growing old and grey with each other. This starts to become as exciting as watching paint dry. After this, we are told that we need to keep it spicy, interesting or be creative to keep the magic. This becomes a full time job outside of your full time job, and the longer we stay together the more difficult it becomes to stay engaged in each other. This is why we find ourselves connecting with and being drawn to new people that are so interesting to get to know.

We meet someone who we have the excitement of getting to know the unknown all over again outside of the person you see everyday of your life. That person you have kissed until you don't want to kiss anymore, made love in so many creative ways that you crave someone new instead of something new.

This can start with simple flirting on the job to hooking up with someone after the club, anywhere in between. Sometimes we don't know why this is happening or why we enjoy it so much. Marriage has two sides, one of which many do not want to acknowledge.

There are many great aspects of marriage that we like to acknowledge and are very strong reasons to strive for or want in life. It can truly be a great way to live, in holy matrimony with your significant other and if this is what you long for, by any means go after it. Meeting your soul mate and making that lifelong commitment aligned with whatever religion you follow. Sexual freedom with the one you love in hopes of creating a family that you can be loyal to, guide towards a happy life, centering your world around your family, spending every day of your life with a very beautiful someone that fulfills your needs sexually, spiritually and mentally. This can be real; however like all things it cannot be perfect. So we are to compromise or if the pros outweigh the cons, make the best of your situation. But after so many years, the wear and tear that come with fighting to stay together, through our likes and dislike about each other, start to show on the inside and outside. At this point, the picture we had of marriage starts to look different from when we first visualized it; even with everything we liked about the person is still there. If I gave you chocolate and vanilla, your two favorite flavors, whenever you wanted them consistently for a year, the chocolate and vanilla wouldn't taste the same.

This is what happens when you are married; the only thing is that people in the situations view it totally different. The key is to truly make your significant other feel that wear and tear is not happening. You have to ensure that you have a positive outlook on this disengagement that happens when couples have been together so long, and a way to repair this wear and tear or appear to repair it. Your situation through your eyes looks totally different through my eyes; however your eyes are the only ones that count. Some people do better than others maintaining a positive outlook in unhappy situations. This is the reason there are many that stick together throughout the years and so many that decided not to.

Which do you think is better?

- **(A)** Making someone happy 10 years and divorcing on the 11th year.
- **(B)** Making some one happy 1 year and divorcing the second year.

The answer: they both are good because neither **(a)** or **(b)** allowed an unhappy year with their partner.

They both identified what was happening and opted to not keep things going, but let's look deeper. Those who opt to stay and make the best of the situation after the good times, how would you rate them? Being that you would be still in the person's life the 11th and second year of **(a)** & **(b)** situation, it would depend on the perception of the significant other that determines how the situation is rated. If you do a great job assuring that things are going to get better, then the situation is good. But if you do a poor job and your significant other stays to keep you happy or only because they appreciate the effort of keeping them, then it's only a matter of time before the relationship ends. The question is which one will you choose, how is your outlook, how your partners true perception of what you have or what you want or striving for. How do you get answers to these questions? **Watch behaviors, yours and your significant other.**

DISENGAGEMENT

It's been said that 90% of married people are truly unhappy with their situations. Have you ever wondered why? There are several answers to this question because everyone has their own perspective. Many still hold on to the situation because they have grown accustomed to life as they have been conformed to, that change becomes a long uphill walk that no one feels they can take, like putting together the pieces of your life in the form of a 10,000 piece puzzle. Couples grow so close to each other living for and by each other that everyone that used to be in your circle become distant outsides. Life as you know changes and these distance outsider go on with life without you. When you get the chance to be around your girlfriends or your homeboys again, it's an uncomfortable feeling. You feel out of touch with what's going on due to being confined so long into the world of your home life. If it ever gets to the point of being on your on again, it looks scarier than ever to take that leap. There are many things that keep us bound to the marriage that sometimes we allow it to outweigh the emotional and physical disengagement we have with our significant others. The kids become more important than expressing how we truly feel. The assets you have gained together are not easily split into half's or not easy for us to part with. For those who are already struggling financially as a family, imagine what it would be like to be apart. Two separate apartments, or one apartment and one home that needs to be kept, gas, child support, alimony and the emotional stress of being either on bad terms or it's enough to make you say as that old school song use to say" it's cheaper to keep her," or is to keep him.

After growing close and depending on each other as a team, it keeps you thinking about how convenient things were and ask yourself, "Is leaving this person worth it? Now rich people won't be able to relate to this due to financial issue are not issues to them. This is why the divorce rate in Hollywood is so high. I refuse to believe that the tabloids or the media could make you leave, if you are famous and married to someone famous, living together in marital bliss. Working as a team, spending countless time with each other with no infidelity, then what someone types up in a newspaper or say on TV will not have an effect on the marriage. But if there are any doubts, any infidelity on any physical or emotional disengagement, they can bring one article with a piece of the truth in it, and it would ruffle some feathers in the home. Inside Addition would cause a verbal fight in the house. But if money is not an issue in the picture, the divorce rate might grow from about 40% to 70% in a matter of months. Imagine being able to say, "Anything my significant other wants in the divorce, they can have it" then divorcing someone would come without a second thought.

You would pay whatever to be away from that person. But people who are living in the regular world don't have that luxury. We have to penny pinch and struggle to get by in everyday life, making our pockets the most sensitive place that we can be kicked, more sensitive than your nuts, for a guy. Women get so use to the comfortable life provided by a stable environment that marriage can be, that they realize that it may not be easy to have it this good again. So they hold on, fuss, argue, fight, and make up. They put up with some abuse, verbal and physical, as well as infidelity as long as the man brings the money and spend most of his time at their home.

They weigh the pros and the cons and do whatever it takes to keep the other person. In men and women this is true, which is why if you have ever broke up with or divorced someone, you may have experience an ex, that does whatever they can to be around or destroy any plans you may have of succeeding and being happy without them. This is where baby momma/daddy drama comes in the picture.

It's the reason you hear, "if you divorce me I will take you for everything! Or the guy that feels "if I can't have her no one can."

We have to realize that life is a journey that includes a series of falling down and getting up. There is going to be hurt, there is going to be happiness. Joy and pain we have to realize that these emotions are only a state of mind. We make them tangible; we make them affect us in physical and emotional ways. We don't eat, we don't sleep, we hurt ourselves with drugs or we eat ourselves into obesity. We hurt ourselves physical and sometimes we kill ourselves, literally, all in the name of a state of mind, a perception of someone. Usher recorded the record "Let it Burn", which represents that hurt but low and behold the burning is temporary and it don't last forever, we have to stand strong, face it and overcome it. We have to want happiness for others as we want it for ourselves. We should never want to be the sole reason another human being is unhappy or happy. This is another form of a power trip; because it is a powerful thing to control some ones emotions and many human being want the power, selfishly seek that power.

Are you selfish?

We need to view break ups and divorces as growth. Sometimes we outgrow each other and to ensure that you reach that level you are destine, its healthy to part ways with those who feel you should not grow.

What about a cleansing period because sometimes our mates outgrow us. We are happy at a stable state when they are not, so we need to cleanse our life of those that don't want to be in it, the way they were in it initially. We should not get emotionally wrecked by something that would truly make us happy, make us stronger and cleanse us in the long run. I understand this is difficult to grasp, due to us being taught since we were kids to act a certain way when we feel hurt. We hold grudges towards those who are not favorable to us or don't have our best interest at heart. This is not to say be emotionless, but it is to say that these emotions are not supposed to control us. They are not to be in charge because your emotions belong to you, you don't belong to your emotions. As a wise man once told me, "this energy in motion is going to be and has always been the death of the human being". We expect those we outgrow or those we are no longer interested in to simply understand and get over it, but when the shoe is our foot we don't want to get over it. We make the situation so much different but it is truly the same. Breaking up to make up again is a game of regression, fear of letting go of the past and embracing the future, even if it shows that you will be alone for a while. This is the cleansing and growth period you should take seriously because it is to get yourself prepared for the next encounter. Take this time to learn from past mistakes and prepare for future improvement. Some of us are happy with the way we are because that's how it has always been. If you are happy with the way things used to be, then it's clear that you are living in the past. I know it feels so right when things are comfortable for you that you do whatever to get that feeling back, if you ever lose it. But our lives are thrown off course purposely. Your world is turn what many calls "upside down" because you have out grown it or when you attempt to combine your world with someone else's world, there is no room for both.

We need to be able to identify when these times in our life comes and be able to handle this transition without running from it. This will only prolong the inevitable or have you spending a large part of our lives in situations of unhappiness or just settling for what we have.

There are situations where we can settle for the person we have out grown and we go on to be together forever. Marriage, children, growing old together, and this is a beautiful thing. It is as long as you are truly happy with the situation and not involving others in your circle or does not have any need or want to include anyone else in your circle. Your situation is great as long as this is your perception of it. There are many who are in situations and they are as happy as ever, so they don't understand or can't perceive how others are not aligning themselves with what they feel is right. They frown on relationships outside of the significant others, husbands, wives, etc. they speak out against this strongly. This is totally understandable, as long as you are being honest with who you are, how you feel and that which you speak out in support of and against. If it's real, then it's real. It's a beautiful thing to see two individuals that have been together for a long time and they still date, hold hands, and other intimacy are still alive in the union. Being able to look at someone you have spent the last 10 years or even 5 years with, and still have that brand new feeling about them. When vows are renewed after 50 years of marriage and you both exchange a kiss that contains just as much electricity the kiss at your wedding day. The thought of two individuals so attracted to each other sexually that they strive to stay active and in shape so they are sexually adventurous to keep sparks flying. Two attractive individuals that understand where each other wants to be, and who they want to become that they continue to grow together. Many are envious at what they have; true focus on each other in a world of so, many distractions.

They both have to understand where they have been, where they are and where they want to go or become. It's okay to start from two different backgrounds, it makes it that much interesting to get to know each other from the path you both took a journey down to get to where you are now. It's great to be on the same page or run in like circles naturally in order to really understand each other. This understanding as well as open communication then leads to an over standing of this individual while you each communicate where you both want to go.

This is a very important piece of a relationship and can make and break your relationships. We grow so close to whom each other are as oppose to whom we see ourselves as. This makes us out grow each other until we move on to different partners ready to pick up where the last left off. This can be prevented by having a clear vision of your partner's vision of themselves when this happens; it helps what you have, be able to stand the test of time through the turbulence or bumps in the road that ends so many relationships. Things that end other people's relationships would not interfere with what you have and many will look on in confusion trying to find out why. The both of you go on to marry or bring kids in the world, but still maintaining a strong connection and over standing. This is the picture that inspires us to inspire others to strive for. We have to understand how to identify the level your partner is on where they are and want to go. When this information is not clear, the foundation of what you have is easily broken. There is always one of these elements missing in relationships that fail. Think back at your past relationship and you may identify where you went in the wrong directions causing a failed union.

IN LUST WITH YOU

Have you ever been in love with another person? Have you ever felt that another human being on earth completes you? Have you ever felt excited at the mere site of someone or the thought of getting the chance to see someone? There is certain electricity you feel when you embrace that person, kiss that person. Anticipating the next time you can be with this person before they ever leave your presences. You hear a certain love song and can't help but think about them and how they make you feel. There is no place you will not go with this person mentally or sexually and you could actually see yourself spending the rest of your life with them. The phrase I love you professed with so much confidence, eagerness, and conviction that every time you say it, it gets stronger and stronger. Sometimes you really don't like to see her interact with other guys, being that you are a guy, she is beautiful and you see that look in their eyes. Sometimes you don't like when he interacts with other females because you are a woman, he is very attractive and you know how women are. When you are out and the opposite sex makes an attempt at you, the only thing you can think of is how lucky you are to have them. The mere thought of your significant other accepting offers, or making attempts with someone other than you makes you very angry and makes you feel betrayed. The thought of your woman engaging in flirtation, kissing or sexual acts makes you feel disrespected to the point of wanting to put her in her place. If not verbally, then physically, or better yet putting the person in their place who is involved with your significant other, verbally or physically. If this doesn't ease or comforts you, thoughts of harming yourself may enter your mind to hopefully gain the compassion and attention of your significant other. In hopes of taking the attention away from the other person they are involved with outside of what you two have until the point of harming them and yourself.

If you feel anything like this or close to it, you are not in love; you are in lust with that person. Even though, one of the L words are used 90% of times more than the other in our everyday social life, the one that is used less seems to overshadow. The meaning of the word love has been used and abused until it really has become a multi context word. It can be used in five different sentences and mean about five different things. We can say it and mean it this way and a person can hear it, yet take it that way. We wonder why the "Game of Love" as many refers to it can be confusing, unpredictable and frustrating to many.

We must understand that the words we used to express ourselves define the perception of our character as well as impacts the way our expression is received. If we are not building and constantly growing our vocabulary then we are hindering our growth as people. We really need to find other words to express this feeling of so call love we processes for each other, to ensure the way we express it is clear to those we are expressing it. This will aid in understanding the level our significant other are on at the time we meet and help them understand the level we are on. It also helps with communication with our significant other that we have spent long periods of time with in order to ensure we can. If we like to continue what we have, simply leaving no reason for assumptions is the key of redefining the definition and word choice to help us all dwell in more of a harmonizing fashion.

We don't love our girlfriends like we love our sisters, yet the way we feel about them is expressed using the same word. Then throwing in your love for your father, love for your friends. What about how much you love GOD. Love in so many different ways but it's all the same word. There is so much room for confusion.

We should all learn to care about each other, first and foremost. Throw love out of your vocabulary, conditionally and unconditionally. If you are about people, you will not hate people, if you care, then you wish for and want the best for people always. This love you have for your significant others, replace it with care. The reason, because of you caring for him or her, you will react totally different, if they decided to break up with you.

You wouldn't be an emotional wreck because if you care then you would respect it, and sincerely want the best for that person if they are with you or not. If you decided to leave your significant other, you would be able to and still be willing to help that person out at times. And the other person would respect your decision. However, love is too big for human beings. In love, emotions become difficult to contain. You have to fight the feelings or allow your emotions to run wild. This is when we do things we regret for the rest of our lives, all because of love.

NICE & COMFY

There comes a time in relationships where couples grow close together, become disengaged, and break up to give each other space. We get fed up with each other and call it quits, or sometimes we work it out and get back together. Many consider working it out due to going back to the dating scene, only to find that getting back out there is not that easy of a transition. They drift slowly back towards the person they have grown comfortable with being around, hanging out with and having sex with. The one they clearly understand and has grown tired of yet is the most predictable. This is the foundation of many relationships today.

It has been said that relationships are two people that can and will put up with each other on a consistent basis. There are many things that we will accept or deal with from a special someone that we wouldn't from another person. This is "love" that many of us feel for each other. This is the "love" that many of us are hoping to one day have that they will cherish. Having a mate that will never leave you, no matter what obstacles that get in your way, is what many yearn for.

There was once a beautiful chic that I knew who got involved with a guy. She allowed him to take her out, wine and dine as well purchase her nice things. He did things for her that a good boyfriend would do and was there for her anytime she needed him. This went on for several years until their relationship started to hit the period where being around each other became a little less exciting. They were open to many things to spice up the relationship, because after all, they could see themselves getting married one day.

Time started to take its toll making them start spending time away from each other which was natural for love birds at this point in the relationship. They trusted each other and communicated, which is what is needed in a good relationship. They didn't notice that there was a change happening in their situation due to being totally focused on the fact they had an ongoing relationship, which was not what a lot of their friends could say. This made them feel very lucky to have each other, and very happy that they met. They knew each other's friends very well and have had countless dinners and holiday parties with their families. Each of their family knew, liked and accepted them so this was a match made in heaven.

The focus on how the relationship looked on the outside made them unable to see that there were some things that had changed. The movie dates were not as common, the conversations became shorter. Time spent with each other became shorter based on the feeling of being around one another so much, made them feel space was needed. So there were a few more ladies nights out and hanging with the fellas that was happening. However this wasn't an issue because they did make their way back to each other. When they did, sex became a little routine than usual and they became very used to their bodies. She had a clear understanding of what he likes and he knew exactly what she liked. They gave each other exactly what they liked until it became predictable. This made the sex become less frequent, going from 5 times a week to one to two times a week. Later on, less frequent than that. This is where things became weird because now the occasional flirting they dealt with when they were out with their friends went from flirting to holding a conversation at the club or pool hall. Accepting that drink that a flirter offered to buy, dancing with the chic in the sexy dress and even exchanging numbers.

This resulted in much more as you probably could imagine, and there, only one thing that would eventually happen. She finds a phone number, he checks her text messages, she calls and he does not answer and he shows up at her house very late yet she is not there. Then soon followed confrontation, allegations and fighting. Trust issues took its toll on the couple and the young lady found herself in a frustrating position. She was almost at a point in her life where she would be settling down, getting married, having kids and planning a future. She had the perfect life plan set to where she could be ready to have their 2 kids off to college and still be young enough to maintain a fun spicy relationship with her husband. Travelling the world, shopping, vacations on the beach, etc. She now finds herself dealing with issues she only hears about from some of her frustrated friends and unhappy co-workers. She felt so far away from those situations they dealt with, only to find her front and center with a guy who feels he needs another chic to satisfy him in a way she thought she could. She thought she "held it down" in that department, only to find out, not.

One day she was out with her friends and noticed how many attractive guys were always flirting with her. She saw how her friends, some of those who were involved with guys, still played along with the flirting with no worries of anyone catching them in the act. This made her feel like she was still young and that she didn't have to sit around worrying about this guy that she had grown to love, not wanting to be the man she felt she deserved. So she did the obvious at this point. She called her man over to have a face to face and let him know that it was time for them to go their separate ways. This was not easy but she felt it was best for her. She took a little time off from hanging out due to the emotional decision; however she was back out on the scene with her friends and ready to mingle. She dated a few guys, flirted and hung out late. She shared funny stories about her encounters with her friends and looked forward to meeting new guys. This was all for her to move towards making her decision as to who she would take serious that could take her further than her ex. She weights her options only to find that there were issues with the new guys that her ex didn't have. These guys on the dating scene now made her ex look like the gentleman she always knew him to be.

She thought about the times they had and how much she loved him. She thought about the connection they shared and how they seemed destined to be together. She missed the way he made her feel special with his gestures, and how they were the envy of all couples they knew. This made her start asking, what happened? Then it became clear that he was dishonest with her and broke her heart being out his friends. She thought about him cheating with another chic given her the love he swore she would only have access to, betrayal. This made thing for her that much more confusing because she found herself thinking about him more as the weeks passed. One day she was at a restaurant, dining along on her lunch break and to her surprise, look who comes over to say hi. This was a special moment that she couldn't let him see her become excited over. She had to watch him and play her cards cool. He was unexpectedly excited to see her and he told her how much he missed her. He told her how he is always thinking of the times they spent together and how much he loved her. He also told her he thought about the connection they shared and how it's seemed they were destined to be together. He let her know that he missed the way she made him feel special and how everyone compared their relationship to the most successful and envied relationships.

At this point she is ecstatic, but she stays calm. She lets him know that it was nice to see him, left a tip and advised him she would see him around. He then asked the question she had hoped, "can I call you sometimes?" She replied sure. Now it was time to give him the impression that things are going great and that she is on the dating scene having a blast. The first few times he calls she allows the calls to go to voicemail. She would reply with a text, indicating she was busy and would try to call him back later. She would say this while sitting at home alone on Saturday night due to not wanting to go out on the dating scene. After playing around waiting for the right time to engage her ex, she was out running errands and saw her ex at the traffic light going the opposite direction. She looks closer to see that there was a very attractive young lady on the passenger's side of his car. She looked very happy and she was laughing hysterically at something he said to her. She immediately thought about how he made her laugh. This made her realize that it was time to get her man back. She saw that due to her dodging his phone calls, that he had stop calling over the past week so she made the attempt to reach out. This time she got his voicemail. She became discouraged and felt that he was busy with the attractive chic she saw him with.

She spoke with her friends and told them how much she miss him, and they were advising her to get over him. She talked to her mother and her mother saw it in her eyes that she missed him and encouraged her to talk to him. So she did reach out again. They talked and decided to meet up. He was his normal charming self, however this was due to him feeling really bad about how things went when they broke up and he was determined to get her back and treat her right. But what he meant by treating her right was, being very careful with the decisions he made that could hurt her. He really did not like hurting her so he vowed he would do anything to protect her if he could get another chance. She did feel he was being truthful and opted to give him another chance. She felt that the fact that she left the first time should let him know how serious she was about him being truthful and loyal and that she would leave again. She felt this was enough to make him respect her. They started things off slow but eventually saw themselves picking up where they left off. Being in love and having fun. But, all fun things come to an end just as theirs did. The infidelity showed its ugly face again in their relationship and she was livid. She felt this was a road they had gone through and she wanted him to know that she was not having it.

She did realize that she did not want to go through the situation again, and not just the flirting with other girls. She also did not want to go through the break up and dating scene again, so at this point she weighted her options. After they were done fighting, she realized how whenever she put her foot down she got respect from him. She was able to make him comply whenever she had to put her foot down, she thought, this may not be a bad situation. She does love the guy, she's used to being around him, having sex with him and she can make him comply when she saw that he was moving in the direction she didn't want him to go. She realized that there will always be issues but she would rather deal with issues from a man that she can get to comply as oppose with one whom she could not. She found herself on the dating scene with guys who did what they wanted to do when they wanted to do it. So she is now happily married to her ex, in which they went on the have those two kids. They are still together till this day raising their kids. However she still realizes that the relationship she has is not perfect but she has a man that loves her and will "act right" to make her happy. So what more could she ask for?

This is a familiar situation many relationships are built on. The nice and comfortable relationships that go on to become marriages or just lifelong lovers that sticks together without going down the aisle. Don't get me wrong, there is nothing wrong with this fact. It's all about what 2 people feel is best for them. Others don't have to support because none of us needs approval from anyone on our decisions we make in our love life.

We must understand that this nice and comfy situation could become a problem in the future, to where one of you recognizes this, and want more. I have saw where one of you decides to take a walk outside of the safe zone and test the waters. They realize that life is short and that despite having a loving relationship at times with this person; it may be time to step out. However there is also the part where this happens yet the two of you remain together hiding it from each other. There is also the part where the infidelity does not happen and you both stay with each other in misery, knowing that the situation is still standing due to neither of you wanting to start over. This can be a problem in relationships that many don't want to deal with, or choose to deal with yet stay together.

It is very important to understand that the statement, all we need is each other as a couple, is not true. We have to understand that we are influenced by those who we surround ourselves with, which can determine the direction of your relationship with your lover. We can be in this comfortable situation, and all of sudden find ourselves attempting to try new things, or reaching for something new outside of the relationship. Many preachers have advised their congregation to beware of whom you associate yourself with or, beware of who you allow in your circle. I think this is true, but let's look at from a realistic angle. You can surround yourself with the so called right people, but what difference does it make if you are not happy? What if you don't like the people whom you have to associate with to not hang around those that will make you do what you really want to do? If you have to force the situation, set your lifestyle up to ensure the situation stays strong, is it really strong? Are you really nice and comfy, or are you at a point where you are waiting for things to fall apart?

CIRCLES

If you drew a circle, you would notice that whatever is inside the circle is fully surrounded, and protected. If you take positive energy, a good feeling or confident feeling, place it on the inside of a circle, this energy will continuously feed off itself becoming stronger and stronger, due to no negative energy from the outside getting in. This is the definition and formula that proves the importance of people surrounding each other with positive people.

Now, take that same circle placing negativity inside of it. Negativity will have a chance to feed off of itself without any positive energy from the outside getting in. This is the formula in which negativity has the environment to grow, and impact any person that comes in contact with it. Keeping a positive attitude can mean the difference between success and failure in business, personal and love life, sports entertainment, etc. To start and end your day on a high would mean a more productive day. To go even further, let's look at the center of the circle as yourself and the outer edge that surrounds the circle, are the people you surround yourself with. They can be friends, family, associates, etc. If you are a positive thinking individual yet surround yourself with two positive thinking people and two people who deep down don't have the best wishes for you, how will it impact you?

First and foremost, you will need to be able to identify who has your best interest at heart. Here is a simple way. Now we don't want to get into labeling people you know or have known for a longtime as negative, but just focus on the facts. Do not focus on their behaviors; look closer at your behavior. What mindset are you in when each one comes around? What activities are you partaking in, in their presence? What exactly do you and these individual talks about when you are amongst each other?

While you are doing and saying things that you say and you do with them; look at what you are doing and talking about and ask yourself, is this helping or hindering me from being a better me? Determine what you want a better you to look like, and see if you are working toward that, who motivates you toward it, hinders you from getting there. This will make it a little easier to determine the people you should have in your circle. These individuals sometimes turn out to be whom you least expected them to be. It could have you realizing one day that you are connecting with people you would have never thought you would be with. This all comes from you truly focusing on you and what you want for yourself.

Next would be for you to analyze your life to determine whose circle are you in, and do you help or hinder that person's circle. Am I distracting this person from doing what they should be doing or becoming who they can become. Do the people in my circle or whose circle I am apart of have a clear direction of where they want to go? Circles really helps you get your life together or realize the importance of the people we associate ourselves with every day. When it comes to our significant others, or people we are involved with, how are they when it comes to who you have in your circle? They tend to get emotional about whom you may involve in your circle, due to them wanting you all to themselves. However, they should want you to associate yourself with whoever makes you a better you. I know our significant others want to be the only loving, motivating, supporting force in our lives but they must understand that energy does not travel parallel but energy is omnipresent. So, having two people that changed energy between each other makes it easier for other energy, Positive or Negative to interfere. We truly cannot make it alone and no one becomes successful themselves without any help.

Surrounding yourself with the right people, means "Putting your mind to it", to achieve anything. A great mind understands the importance of getting other great minds together to achieve a common goal or vision.

We are all multifaceted people that have different feeling and different types of motivations to keep us focusing and moving forward. What motivates you? What do you need when you are distracted, to get you back on track. This is what needs to be determined so you can set your circle up to effectively work for you. Be exactly who you are and need to be in order to help someone else's circle.

Human beings put the emotion in relationship between significant others. Emotions are what keep us from flying to levels we could reach and change the world. This prevents circles from forming due to our emotions preventing us from having who we truly need in our circle due to jealousy or selfishness. Sometimes the person a man my need in his circle is a beautiful woman, with her head together that motivates you like your girlfriend can't or a very focus guy that truly makes your woman feel like she can conquer the world. Due to their relationship we have to let these individual surround themselves with those who make them want to be better. We as men and women try to include who we need in our circles even if we don't understand the meaning of circles, which causes us to then make decisions based on our emotions that impact each other in unfavorable ways. We become emotionally attached to someone that should only be in our circles and attempts to leave our significant others, making our significant others feel like having the opposite sex in your circle is always trouble.

It can be trouble when emotions are involved. It is difficult for us to understand, over stand, and accept many things that could free us from restrictions. Many kings, queens, actor, entertainers, businessmen, women, and every day people fall due to emotions or the emotion of those close to them. The key is to keep those in your circle that has the best understanding of you and simply want to see you at your best.

Through living your life you will find that these people come in different shape, sizes, colors, and nationalities. They are sometimes outside of whom you would normally connect or associate yourself with, but it is important to put away all prejudices, likes, dislikes, and opinions, anything that ties to an emotion so that you surround yourself with the right circle.

People fluctuate in and out of each other's circle and into and out of new circles throughout life. They are connecting with different people, which is totally healthy for the human race. We have to be open and understanding about this constant changing of people in different circles and not get alarmed. Unlike what we have been taught, there is no loyalty to one circle, because you limit yourself from all the circles you would benefit from or that you could benefit. When you are involved in a positive circle you reap the positive energy there in as well as open a door of opportunity for yourself that wouldn't be if you were not. You can never be successful without helping someone else be successful. You will never get rich without helping someone else be successful. You will never get rich without helping someone else's get rich, you will never get what you want without helping someone else get what they want.

DON'T LOOK BACK

Commitment is the word or term many of us hear, and go in the opposite direction. It is also a vision or thought that many long for, only to get it, and realize it is not what they wanted. The term can be beautiful to the sight when you see an elderly couple that has stuck together for 65 year and still seem to enjoy each other's company, adore each other. But when you probe deep into their lives you may see several incidents of, frustration, arguing, infidelity, violence, and many of the things we would not deal with in a relationship, but we still want the outcome of what the elderly couple has. Many want to go to heaven, but nobody wants to die. Many of us would love the relationship our grandparents have, but not willing to move past the numerous distractions that comes with it. We seem to believe that commitment is a soft easy word that anyone can live by; or live up to. But it is a hard word, a strong word, a string thought and a difficult state of being. We have to over stand that everyone is not going to have it, some of us will be willing to take everything that comes with it, and few of us will achieve it. We have to be prepared for the mistake that are subject to happen down the road of commitment, and realize that regardless of what jumps out on the road we travel, we will continue together. Being prepared is easy to say, because down this road of togetherness, there are monsters that will be revealed to make the strongest or bravest run in the other direction. Commitment is about being willing and able to go through what each other go through and strongly accepting the fact that break ups or divorce is not an option. I heard Will Smith say, "If divorce is an option in your marriage then you will get divorced." Some of us turn back down the road due to them not liking how the road has been, the direction the road has turned, or they see a road with someone else they feel, would be best for them to travel. We don't' realize that some of us truly make each other better people, or challenge us to be the best we can be, before we take that option to give up. We see this better person we can become and become afraid.

We turn back because we feel it's not who we want to be at this point in our lives or ever, for that matter. It is also true that some turn back for other people that enter their lives, wanting what you and this other person may potentially have.

Couples that weather the storm down this road understand a very important fact. If they ever decide to split up, "break up, divorce, then we must not look back. I know this does sound harsh, but to leave each other is a very harsh decision that we have to assume is not made over night. It comes from a series of incidents that brings you to a crossroad. You have to understand that making this decision and looking back later to connect is a mistake. Let me explain. If you leave a person with the option lingering, to get back together with them, then you should not leave the person, only leave when you know you will not consider getting back together, because this will prevent divorces and break ups over trivial things. It will also prevent both sides from not being able to move on due to heartbreaks. If you take away the option of divorce, breakup, then you won't have that as a decision to make. But if you do, then you will know for a fact that it was the right thing to do. If you take away the option of reconciling, getting back together, re-marrying, then you would be less likely to leave each other the things not worth your relationship, as well as if you decide to leave, you will be able to understand that it was the best thing to do and you will move on.

There will be times when we truly don't complement each other, we don't make each other better; as well as the road we started on has turn to a road that is going into a direction that is detrimental to you, physically, mentally, or spiritually. There are many relationships like this that ends, and then reconcile; only to push you back further than you were before. But we reconcile for sexual reason, or fear that we can't make it on our own. Not wanting to see the person with someone other than ourselves. These are all selfish reason to drag our significant others onto situations what benefit yourself only.

This is a huge reason that we must not look back. One thing I have learned in my life time is that the less control you have over your emotions, the more issues and mistakes you will have when it comes to relationships. When I say control of emotions, it's not that I mean being emotionless. You have to show emotions and over stand them, as well as respect the power behind emotions. We have to define love, what it is and what it is not, as well learning to define care. What is the difference between love and care? Love is a lustful disease that spreads and infects us, hindering us from really over standing that it's a selfish state of being. We do things out of love for people because we actually would or don't mind doing it.

So, if I'm in the love with you and I walk from Alabama to Los Angeles to be on your side; I also did it because being by your side is what makes me happy. It makes me feel ecstasy when I'm next to you. Look at this act or situation closely and you will see it's still an act done solely for myself. Conditional love is all many of us can understand, being that conditions is what we can identify with being on the physical plane. Being on earth and being physical beings, it's difficult not to easily connect with physical conditions. When it comes to unconditional love, it's not of this world and its love we should have for our higher source, whatever you call him or it. So if you think about it, anything that we do out of love, in the end, still benefits us. Love makes you turn back, going back to relationship you decide to end for the hope of getting what you want without being with that person. Love blinds you from seeing that even though you really want to be with a person or they express really wanting to be with you, sometimes is not good for either side. If I have taken you through a lot, ups and downs hurt and happiness, I need to see that you don't deserve this. You don't deserve to be hurt. From a different angle, some people are happy and satisfied when their significant others are happy. They really like seeing the person they" love," happy, because that is pleasing to them.

This makes many breakup and then makeup due to the hurt they see the other person going through. So they rekindle the relationship to see the other person smile again, because seeing them smile is pleasing to you. So this is another selfish act that occurs due to the lustful disease called Love. It makes you turn back.

When you care for someone, you will not turn back. You will allow that person to find happiness, no matter, how hurtful it is for you to let them go or how hurtful it is to see them cry, you know they will recover and they will thank you for it in the long run. When you care, you do things for people with no benefit to you. When there is no positive outcome for you, yet you make sure it gets done for someone, that's care. This world needs more care because love being thrown around like a used condom has our emotional state of being in a train wreck. When you truly feel that it's time to move on, do it for the sake of the other person. When you really want to go back and make it work and the other person does, then it makes since. But if you are doing it for the other person or for yourself only, do not waste their time or yours. Care about what going back to them, with you being the person you are will do to them. You know who you are and what you want and if this is the sole person you decide to call it quits with, let it be the reason you decide to leave it there.

THE WORM

Everybody is special in his or her own unique way. There are things about you that I can't say about myself and vice versa. There is something truly special about this woman that I have not experienced with any woman I have met. There may be similarities but this special something gives her a leg up over the girls I have dealt with. I like this about that person, but I like that about this person. Things really start to become interesting when people realize that it's something special that they possess and learn to use it to their advantage. When I say advantage, in this case let speak about this war we call "interacting with the opposite sex or the same sex", whatever your preference. When you realize what you have, unlike any one else, it's natural to work at perfecting it to really improve your chances when it comes to dating. This special something is what I call your worm. What exactly are worms and what are they normally used for? Ask a fisherman. When you are a fisherman, as I discussed earlier, you are more effective at catching what you like however, what also impacts how effective or successful you are, is the bait the fisherman or fisherwoman uses. Some fishermen use worms, others use crickets, raw flesh of other fish, etc. Fisherman use whatever gets the job done. So in the act of dating, it is important for fisherman or all men and women, to have effective bait. Something that is used to attract what you are after.

Some of us use material things as our bait, which has overtime and still does, prove to be effective. Money, cars, clothes, homes, your profession, or the circle that you are affiliated with is used to close the deal. It's true that this is all it takes, especially for men to attract a young "hottie" looking for a good time. It is also important to cast your bait in the appropriate places to ensure an appropriate catch. Example, I wouldn't bet on this type of bait to work in a crowd of rich people. There is also bait that is physical, verbal, and mental. You can attract someone with conversations, physical attractiveness, and wisdom.

Men and women use bait or their worm in the game of relationship every day. We find out our special something, polish it up as shiny as it can be and flaunt it on the dating scene. I know many women with physical worms yet there is something special about each. Be it their eyes, their lips, the silhouette of their upper or lower body, the breast, the skin tone, the butt, and to even the sound of her voice. Women, who I might add, are the best of fishers recognize these attributes and really flaunt them. This is to attract as many fish as quick as they can, only to patiently go through them, measuring what is best for her, throwing them back in the sea until satisfied.

This is the most effective way to fish when it comes to finding that special someone. Men, we are hunters by nature, so even though we try to fish, this comes out. We can have a worm that attracts all the types of fish we want; yet there is no patience involved. There is very little analyzing and throwing fish back. We become intimate with as many as we can, due to our need to conquer. Yet men and women use their worms that we have to be effective for us.

To take it up another level, there are some who take things about them that are not so special and less likely to work as a worm, and turn it into just that. This allows a person to have many worms for all occasions and places, to be effective whenever and where ever they are.

TOYS

There's nothing like your toys, things that are for you and obtained by you base on what you can have. Your toys can complement your taste, your level of living or financial status as well as tell a lot about you. There is also nothing like someone else's toys. Toys of someone more fortunate than you or to get toys you would like to have, but can't for whatever reason. This makes the person who can't have them, come up with any means of getting what they want. An example of this is people who live what is considered "Above their means." If I make more money than you, I am naturally going to have material things I could afford to have that you may not. So you go out scrape, save; sell what you have to get what I have like homes, cars, and clothes. Then there is only so long you could keep "robbing Peter to pay Paul" or living above your means before there is a financial collapse that causes you to lose everything.

When we think about having multiple girlfriends or a number of women we deal with, the average man would consider the man able to do this as lucky. A player or pimp, someone admired. This is still a true feeling. Women are so beautiful, diverse, and plentiful on the planet, out numbering men tremendously. The different nationality, shape, sizes, height, tone, smiles, and personalities, so many to choose from to fit how we feel at different points of our day, week, month, year, different parts of our lives. When you meet someone vowing to be monogamous with them, you have to go out in the world of women and not partake of other beautiful enchanted fruit, like Adam and Eve in the garden. This is a difficult task but there are men in the world that handles this task for years. But there are some that do not handle it so well. This is the reason for so many heartbreaks. When asked why, many of us like to use the excuse of people in the Bible and in Africa having several wives or concubines, but if you take the time to examine this, you will see how similar this is to having toys. Toys always come down to us getting exactly what we want. You can give a child a truckload of toys, but if it's not what the child truly wants, then a truck full of toys is now a truck filled with junk. The toy that men want the most is the ability to see, or talk to whomever we choose whenever we choose. This is a toy that all men can't have, for various reasons; like a commitment to someone already, gift of charm that attracts many women or other obstacles. However, there are some guys who can and does have this toy, men who are most like those in the scriptures who had multiple women. The men that are like most of the men in history who dealt with multiple women, one of the characteristics of these men first and foremost is they are rich, they are kings or men of major accomplishments or men of power and influence.

These are men most likely to get what they want from multiple women and the women themselves are understanding and respectful. Many men want this toy but do not possess any of these attributes. But what happens next, those beautiful shiny toys that we want but don't possess the attributes of those who have it, we find a way to get it. We live above our means, we cheat, lie, spend money we don't have, and go places we shouldn't be to get this toy. Despite the hoops we jump through to get and keep this toy, despite the people we hurt in the process, we still go after it, we still want it. The exact same way we do whatever it takes to stay in the nicest clothes, cars and jewelry to be like those who could truly afford it. We get $100,000.00 cars off the lot when we know we could easily and comfortably afford the 50,000-dollar car. This is natural for people of all walks of life.

The key point to take away is, play with the toys you can afford and are aligned with your lifestyle. This could help men understand and help them stay focused on what they need to be. If you don't have it like a king, you should be focused on getting and building a kingdom, like a king. You have to always be about success to be successful so you can have this toy that many accomplish men are able to have. We have to stop wanting this toy that we can' have. If you go out of your way to get this toy, it only complicates your life more than it would be without it.

FINAL THOUGHT

Men and women go through different stages in life, and I wanted to reveal a couple of stages to help you identify them. This will prevent us from making the same mistakes and falling in an emotional tailspin. The emotional tailspin that causes us to say things we don't mean, to not say what we truly feel, as well as act in a manner that we may regret for the rest of our lives. The physical and emotional damages we cause each other all over the love of ourselves. I want to express love as a selfish disease amongst human but it is only given to truly satisfy ourselves, not the person you are given it to. Like we discussed earlier, if someone I loved moved from Los Angeles to New York and I wanted to be near her so bad, that to prove my love for her, I walk from Los Angeles to New York to be with her. I can't afford a ticket to fly or ride the bus. Some would say this is the ultimate way to show love for that person, but the truth is, I didn't walk to New York for that person. I walked to New York for me and me only, because having that person close to me to shower her with my love, really only benefits me. I would think and hope that she finds my love shower favorable in her eyes, but that's something I may never truly know. One thing I will know is that it makes me feel good to be allowed to shower this person with love. It's what I want to do for you. We must realize that though we go through many stages and have many feelings we must at the end of it all respect what makes each of us happy. If we did this, we would be happy that our significant others sat us down to advise us that the relationship is not working and we need to go our separate ways. We should respect that this is not what they want and if we truly want the best for them, "fighting" for the love we have for someone to convince them we are better for them, is a selfish gesture.

Relationships let me know that we as people try to force them to happen too early in life. As young adults, there are so many things we should be occupying ourselves with other than trying to commit to each other. If we spent our 20's and 30's getting to know us and what we truly want, marriages would last longer and we would truly be marrying a friend. A friend that understands that we have ample amounts of time to know each other as well as know ourselves, and the decision would be mutual. That's why there is so much tension in the air at weddings because no one is sure this is going to work or be the best move at this time. We do want it, but maybe not at this time. Even though the doubt is there, we are encouraged to shake it off. We are convinced that it's just pre wedding jitters. This is what we do because we love that person but it is a selfish thing to do. We are afraid to hurt feelings, so we would rather marry you now and cheat on you later just so we don't hurt you. This must stop if we are going to progress as human beings.

I would like women to read this book for insight on how to handle what a man dishes out during different period of his life. Understanding these level and stages of life we go through can help women see why we do what we do and when we do it. Ladies, it's not about how we think because how we think fluctuates based on the people we are with at the time and the experiences we go through professionally.

This could make me as a man think totally different from another man that may be in the same situation with the same type of girl; however he is in a different place in his life at the time. It also depends on the type of lifestyle that man has lived growing up as it pertains to dating and sexual encounters, and the morals he has. All this has barrens on how we think about situation and react.

I want men to read this book to see that being a player is not what we always thought due to images on TV. I wanted to expose you to the way a real player handled his situations in the single life as well as to reveal that many of us as guys don't have it in us to be a player. Many of need a certain type of woman in our lives for guidance and balance, to ensure that we become the best person we can be, and it's nothing wrong with that. Be true to yourself. If this is the case, then you need to leave this life, marry the girl in your life and live happily ever after.

My experiences with so many women helps me understand and see things the way I do, and I felt obligated to share it with the world. I feel I owe this to you being blessed with the ability to deliver it in a unique way. Truth is only an opinion that many people agree with at a given moment in time. Truth also can change, especially relationship truth, due to the evolution of us as humans continue. What is relationship truth this year, may not be true next year. I am only here to deliver a philosophy called RelationshipTRuth,(spelled this way intentionally) that will plant a seed in your mind and spark the growth of a new way of thinking. The many experiences that I have had, helps me understand the relationships and the powerful role that our emotions have on our relationships when we lose control of them. When we allow what others say and do in relationships to control how we feel, we give up so much of our God-given power to have a healthy state of mind and happy life. This thing we call love has such a huge impact on people being happy with their selves, which impacts how they view and handle things in their everyday life. I give you this for entertainment purposes; however I do feel that it will help many in the process. The vehicle that I will use to launch this philosophy is called the Kennytalkexperience. I have a video blog that I update weekly located at kennytalkexperience.com in which I would love for you to visit. Stay tuned in for more to come from the kennytalkexperience.

I do realize that there will be many to agree to disagree, or just make attempts to somehow discredit the philosophy called #RelationshipTRuth, but know that I don't profess to be an expert. I don't wish to take the place of relationship counselor, doctors or therapist. I'm a man that has a real cool opinion that I was inspired to share with the world.

This book is dedicated to a two very special people, one that has made me feel that anything I aspire to accomplish I can reach, and one that is a motivating force behind me making things happens.

My late brother Antawiaw (Antwan) DeMoss that believed in me when the world including myself doubted me.

My Daughter, Caitlin DeMoss, who motivates me to build a kingdom and leave a legacy for her after I'm gone.

This brand (Kennytalkexperience) is motivated and inspired by the insight, guidance and love given to me by my 2 father figures, Joel Rice and Carl Ivy.

ABOUT THE AUTHOR

Kenneth KennyTalk DeMoss, better known as Kennytalk, Born and raised in Birmingham Alabama. I want to turn your attention the KennytalkExperience, a forum I founded to deliver the new philosophy called #RelationshipTRuth. The reason for the # symbol in front of the word is because this brand started on the twitter social networking site. I started by presenting my followers with the #RelationshipTRuth every day until it grew into the brand that it is today. I wanted to present the world with a book that introduced a new way of thinking to help improve the lives of many that are living in frustration and confusion. I am on a journey that has brought me to this point of using my talents to compose this project and engage others to share their thoughts for the purpose of creating helpful dialogue to help others. This is my purpose. There is so much more to come from this point because there is so much more needed. I believe that I was chosen to write this publication by those in my surroundings that have heard me speak, and realized how helpful this could be to so many. Stay tuned in for more books and information from the KennytalkExperience as well as the video blog I create, Kennytalkexperience.com.

Follow me on Twitter @kennytalkexp
Facebook: kennytalk CMG
Website: Kennytalkexperience.com

www.ingramcontent.com/pod-product-compliance
Lightning Source LLC
Chambersburg PA
CBHW030407290526
45785CB00004B/1928